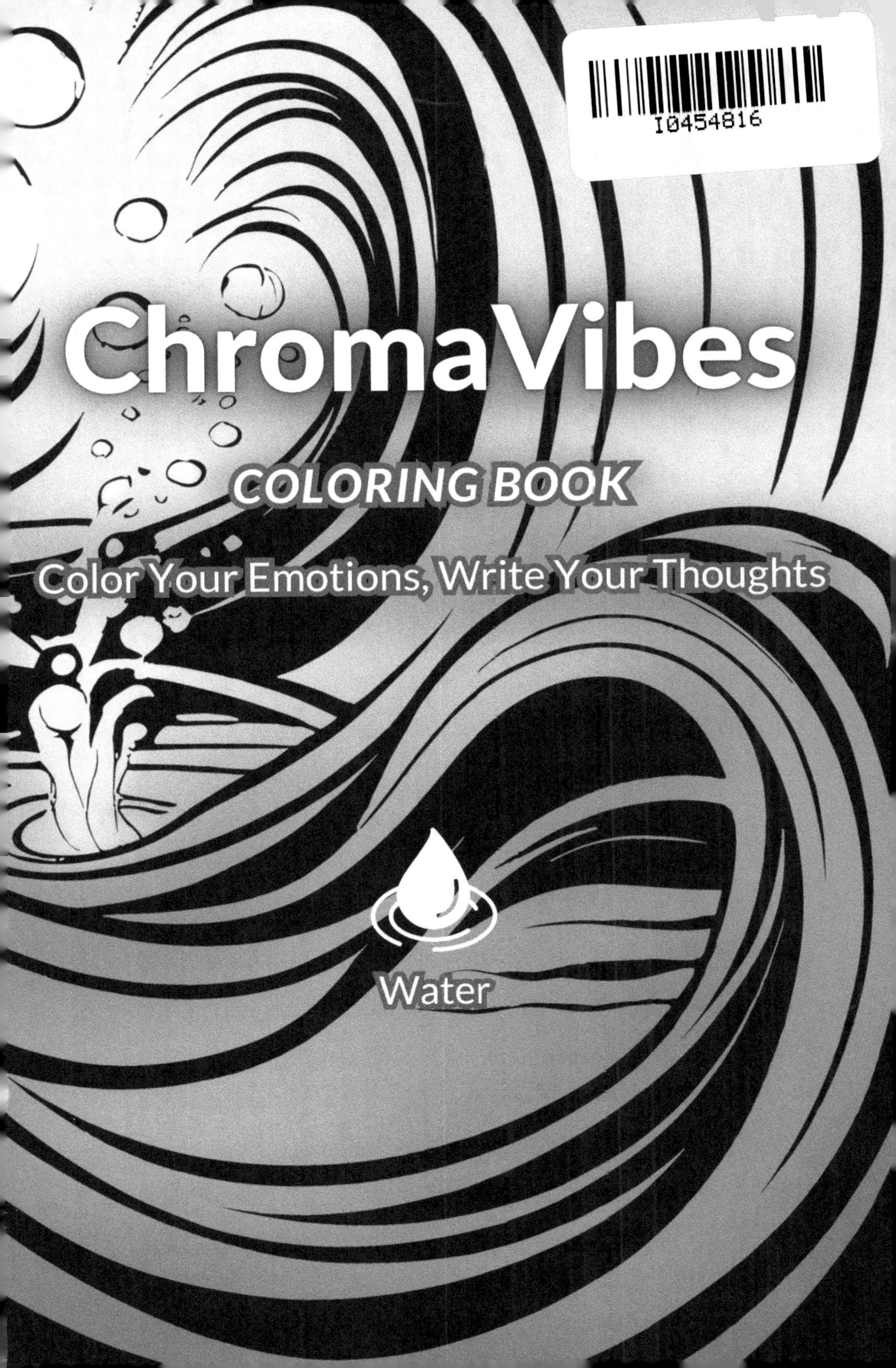

ChromaVibes

COLORING BOOK

Color Your Emotions, Write Your Thoughts

Water

In stillness,
water whispers
secrets of the
universe to those
who listen.

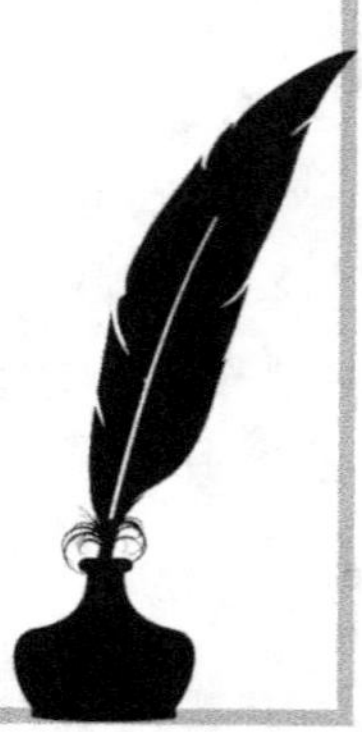

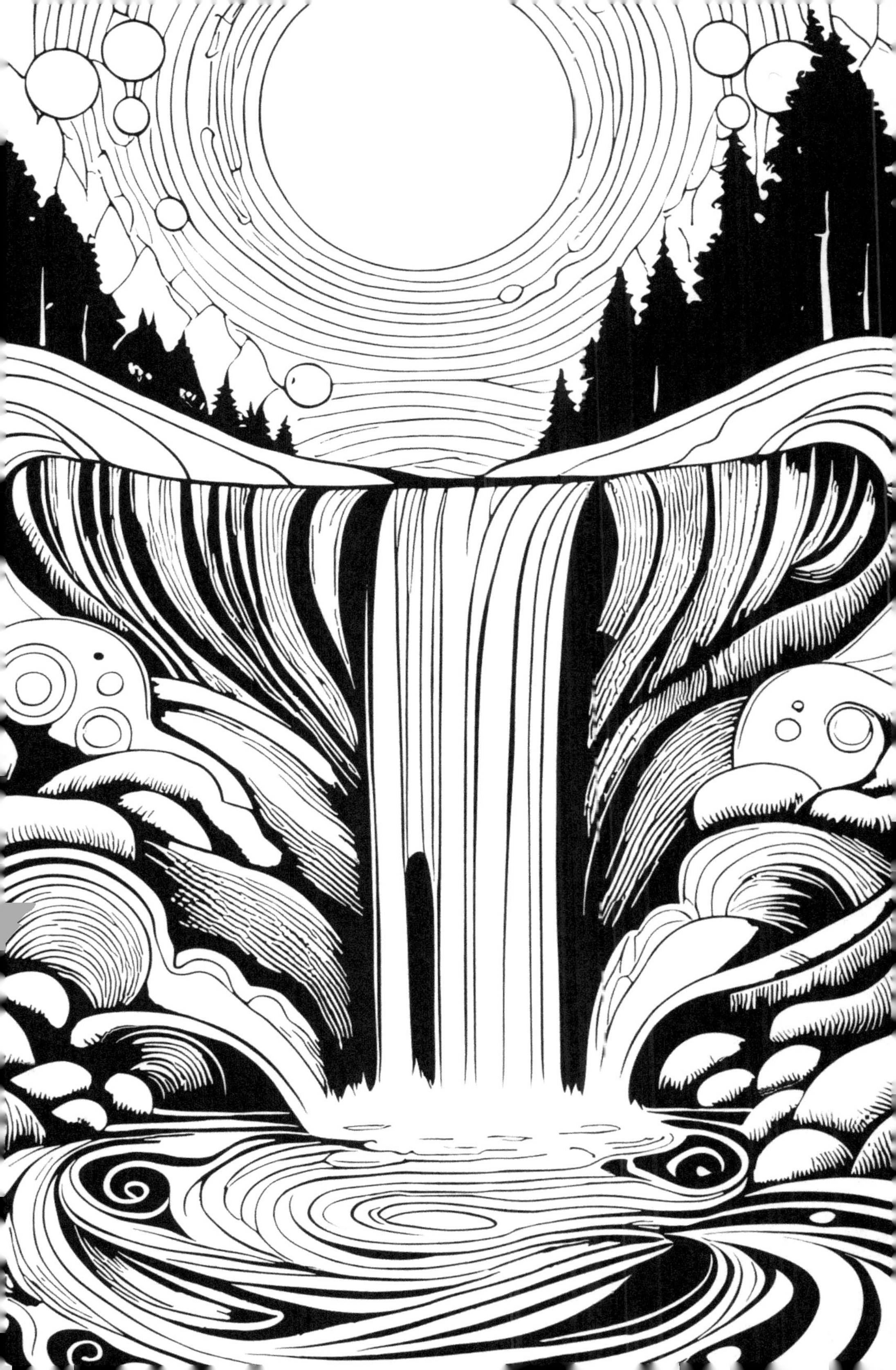

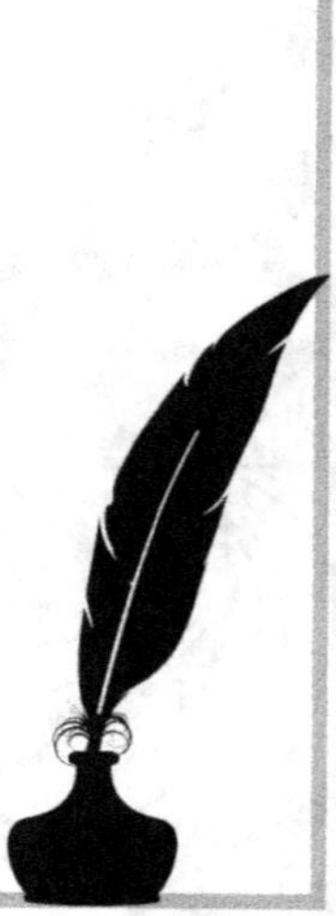

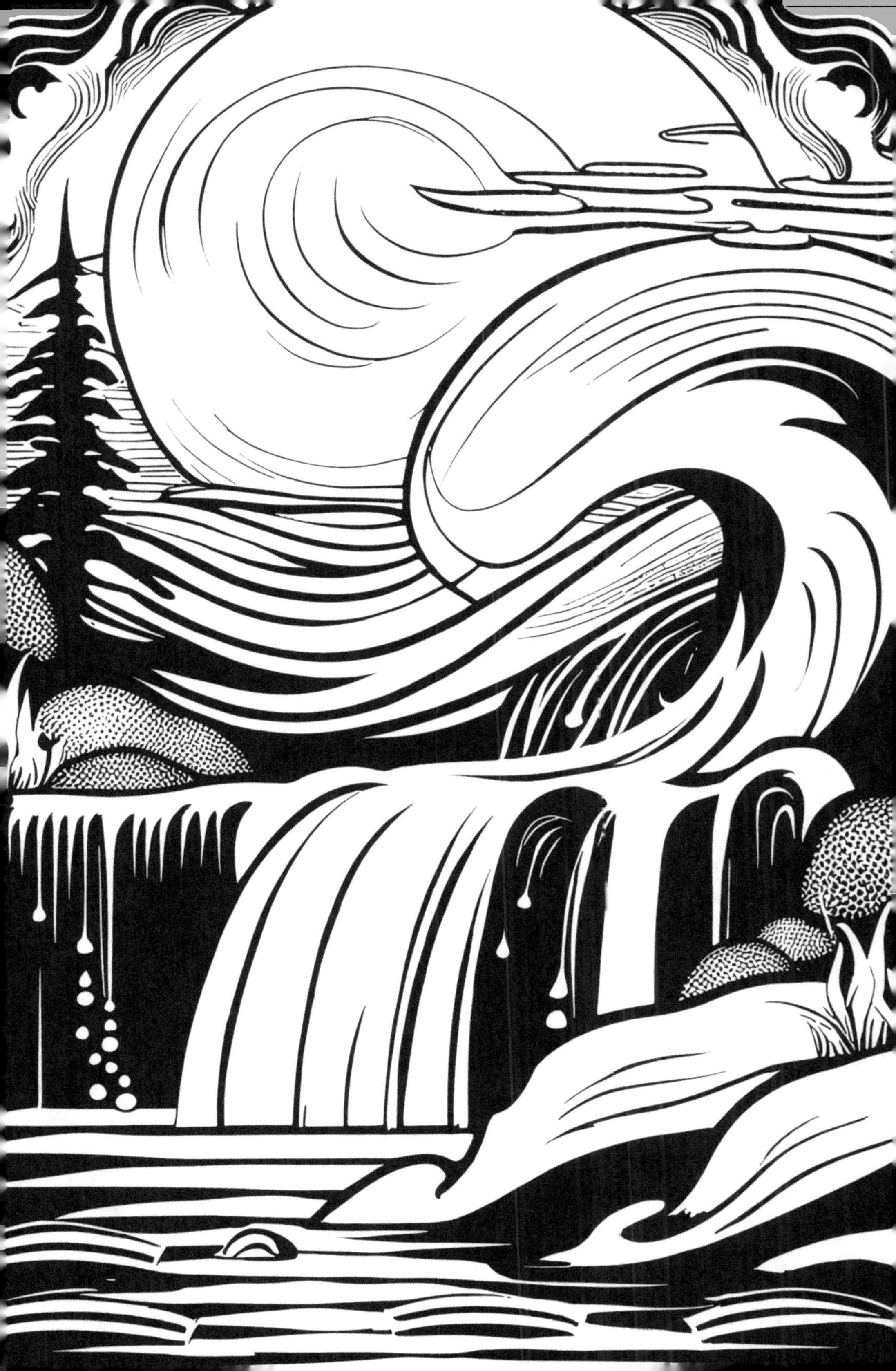

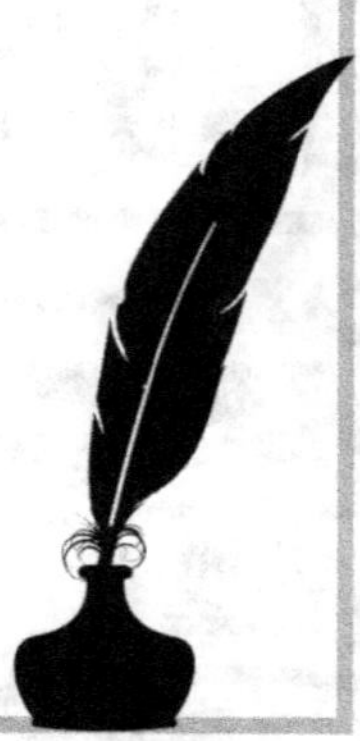

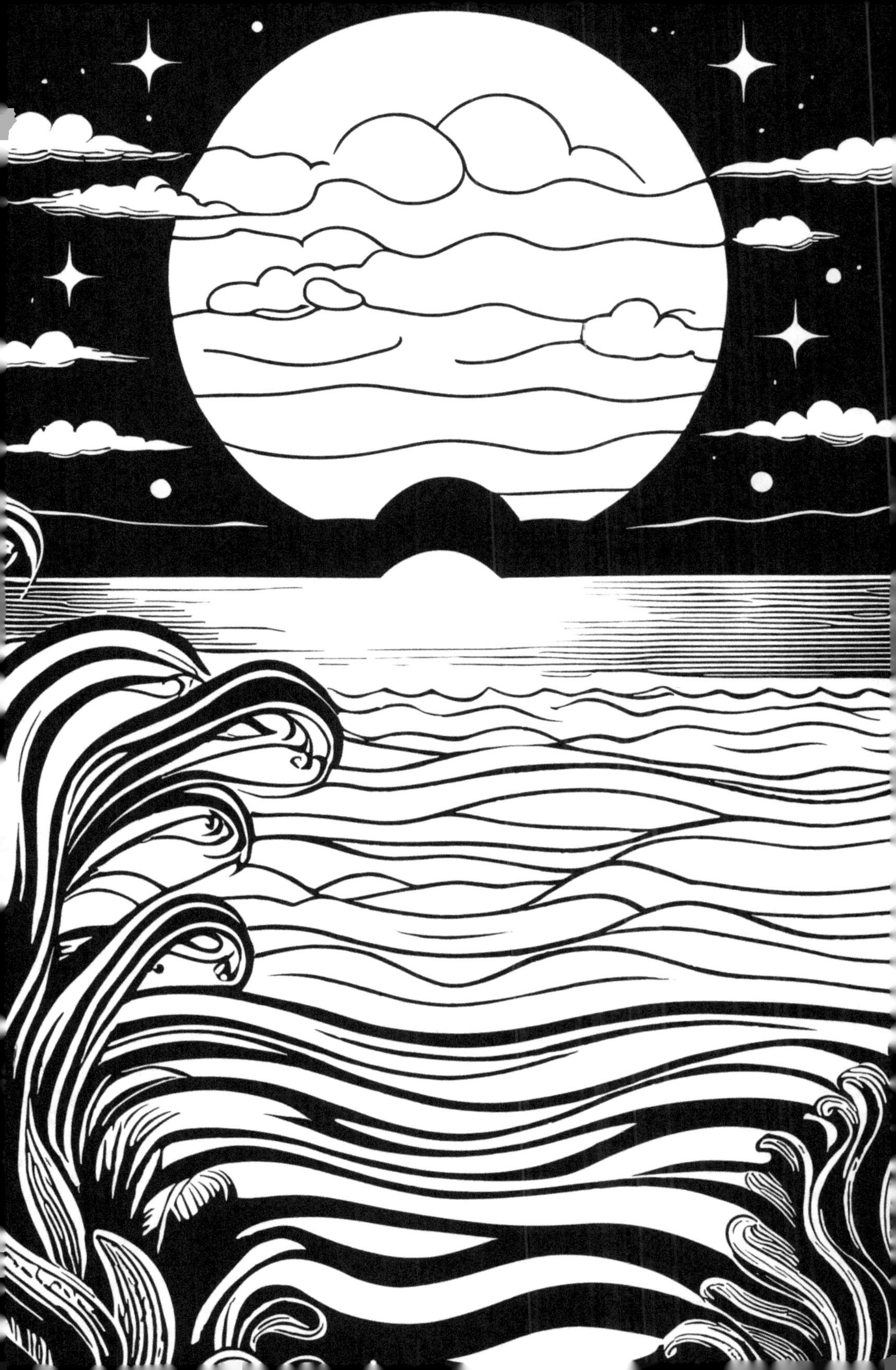

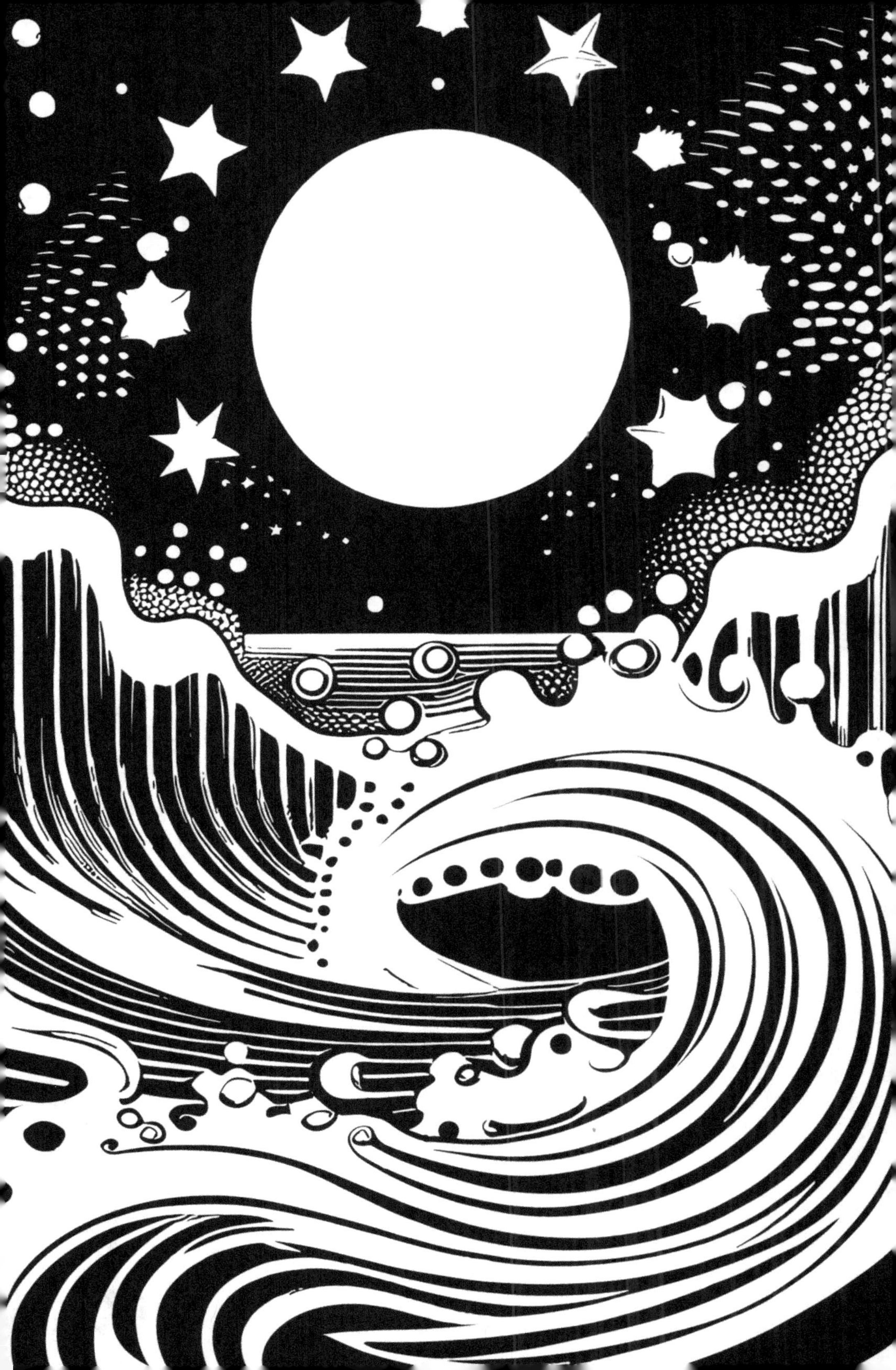

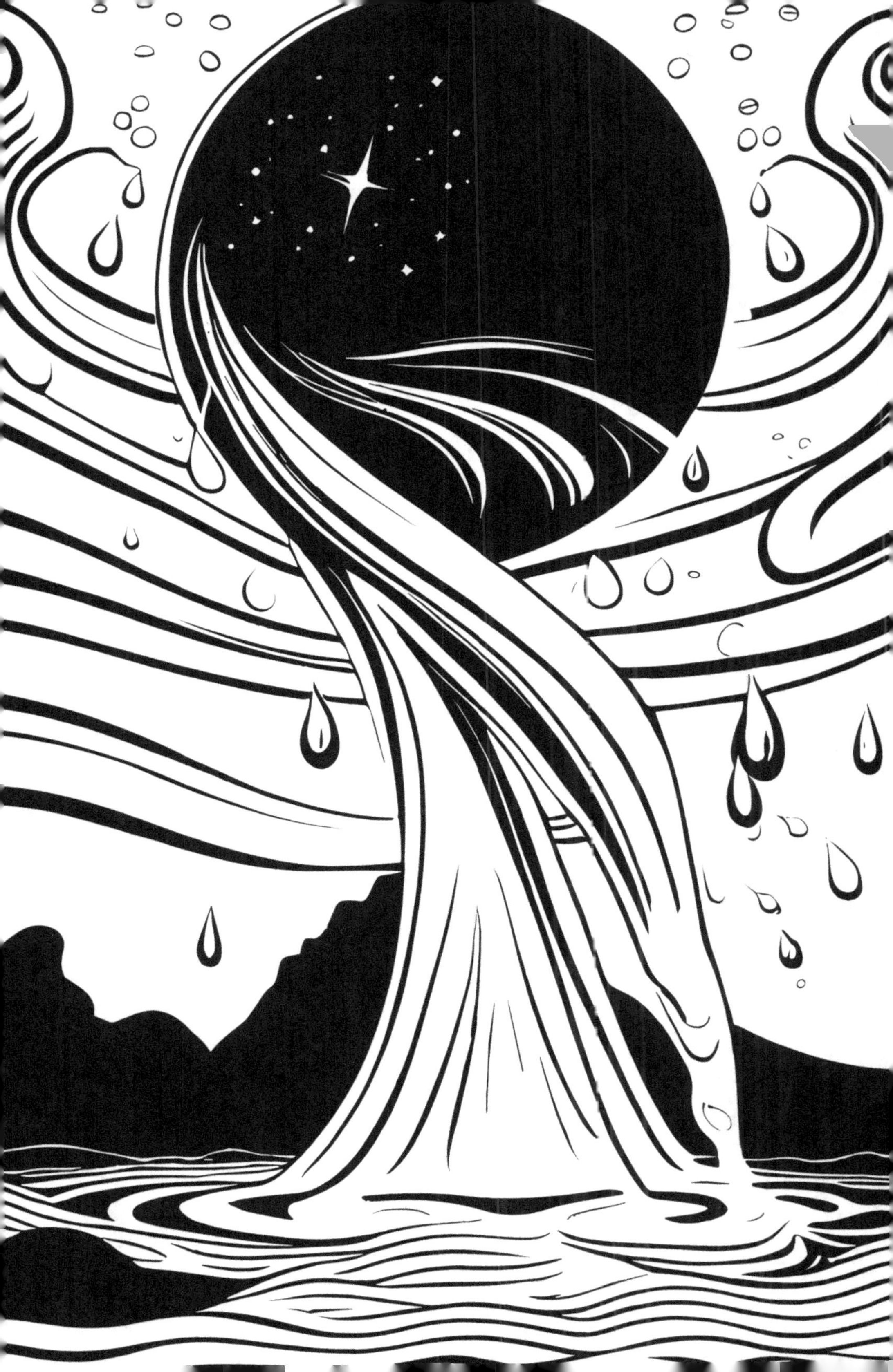

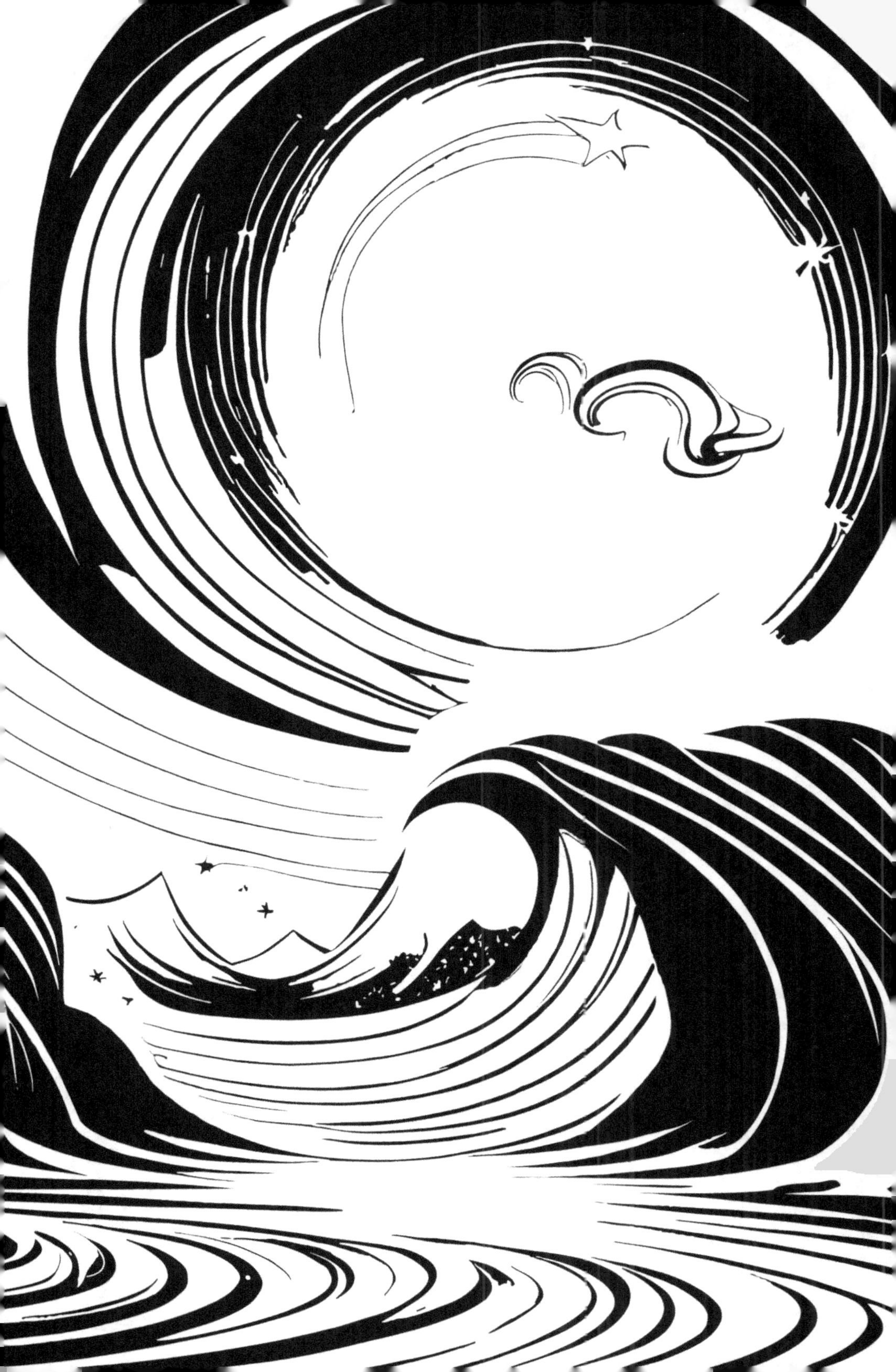

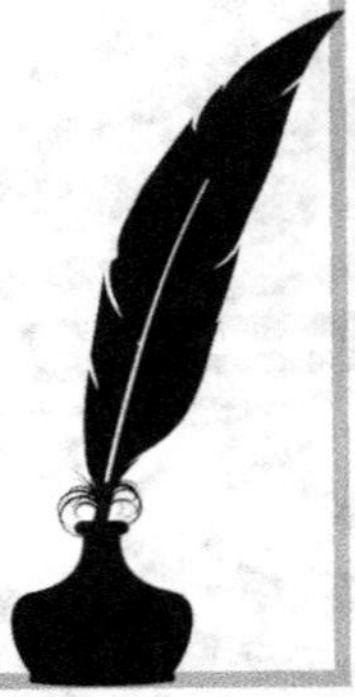

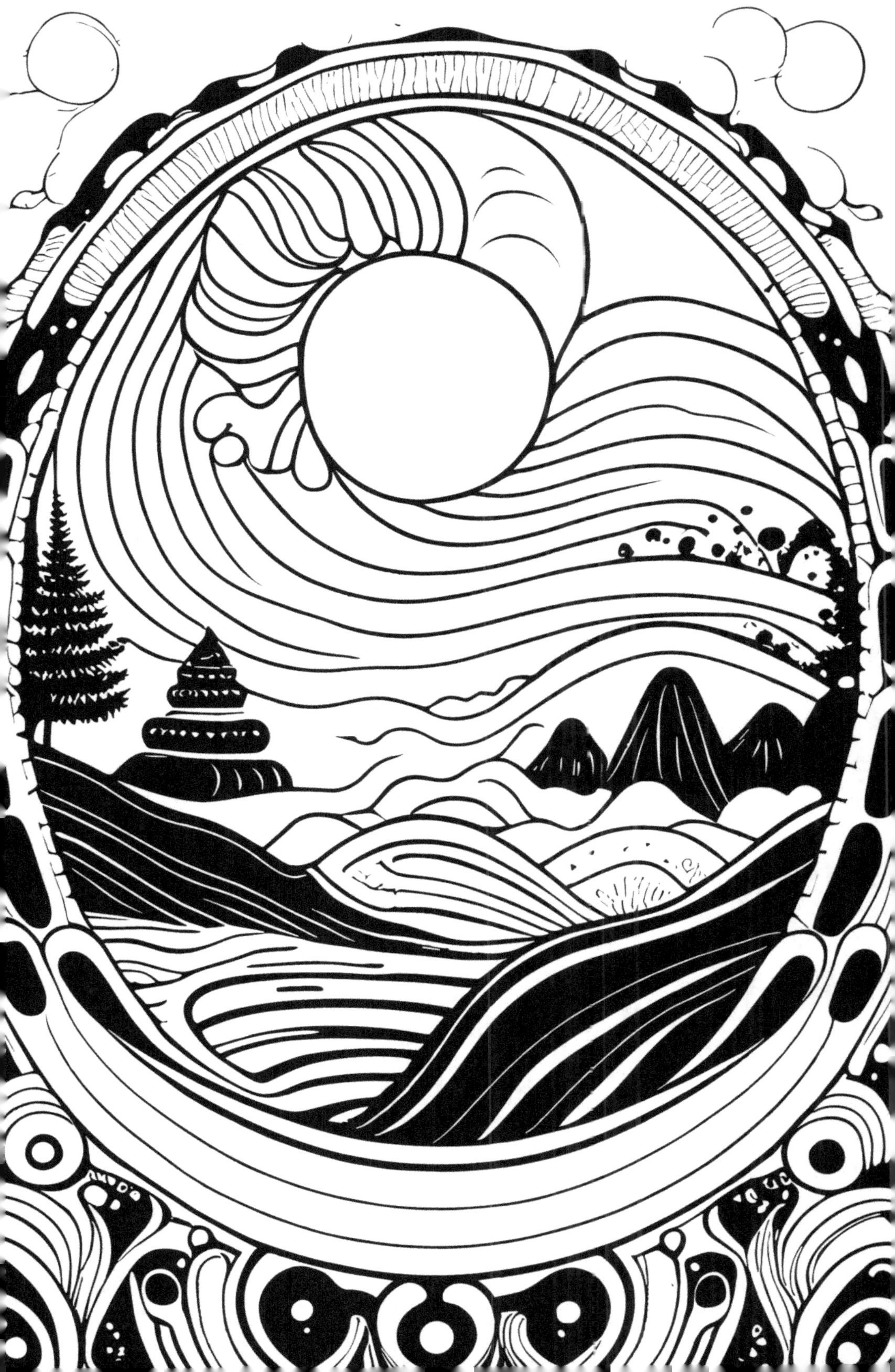

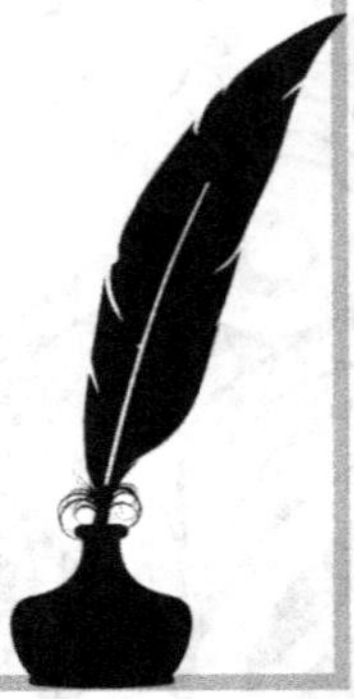

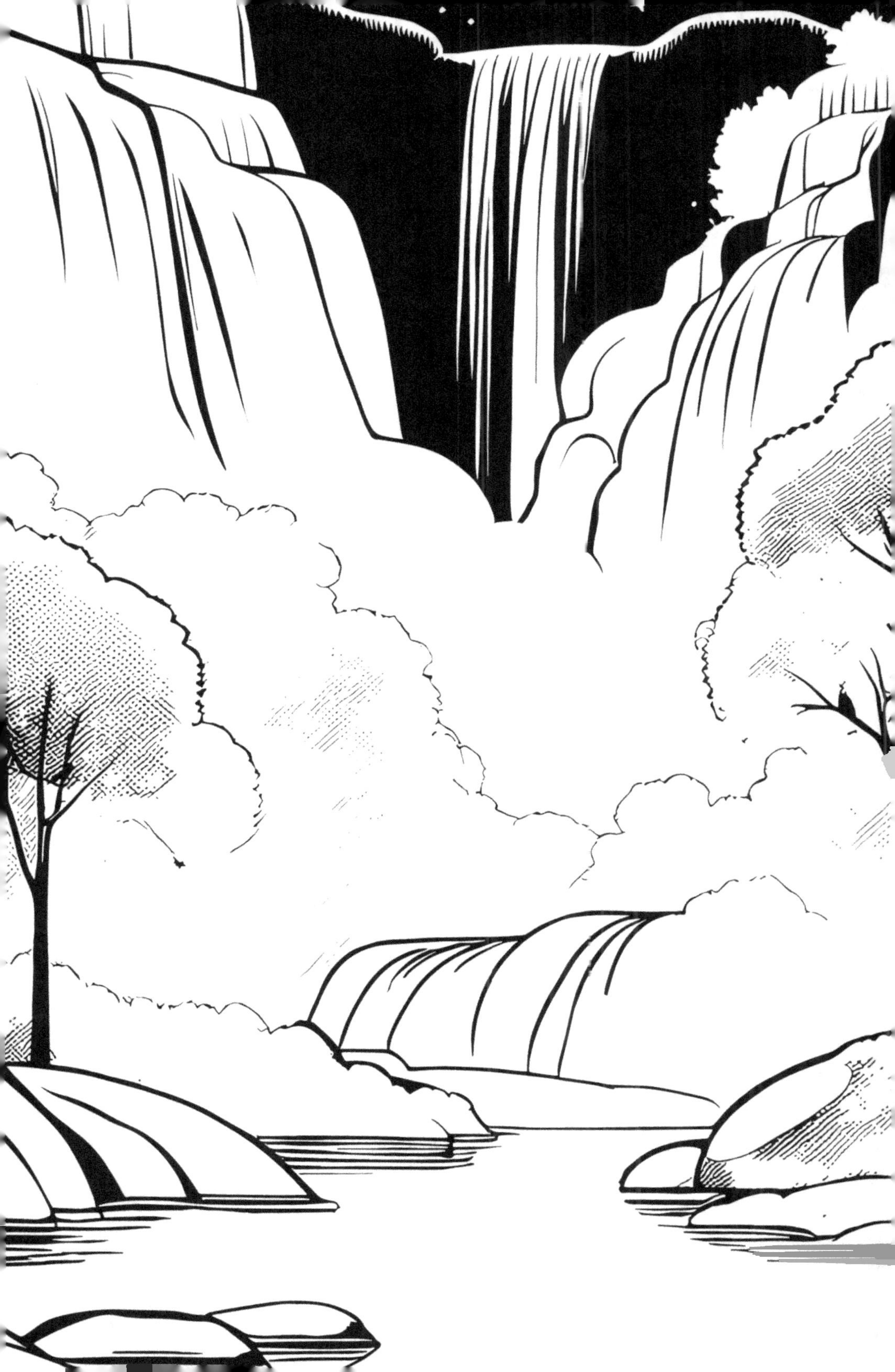

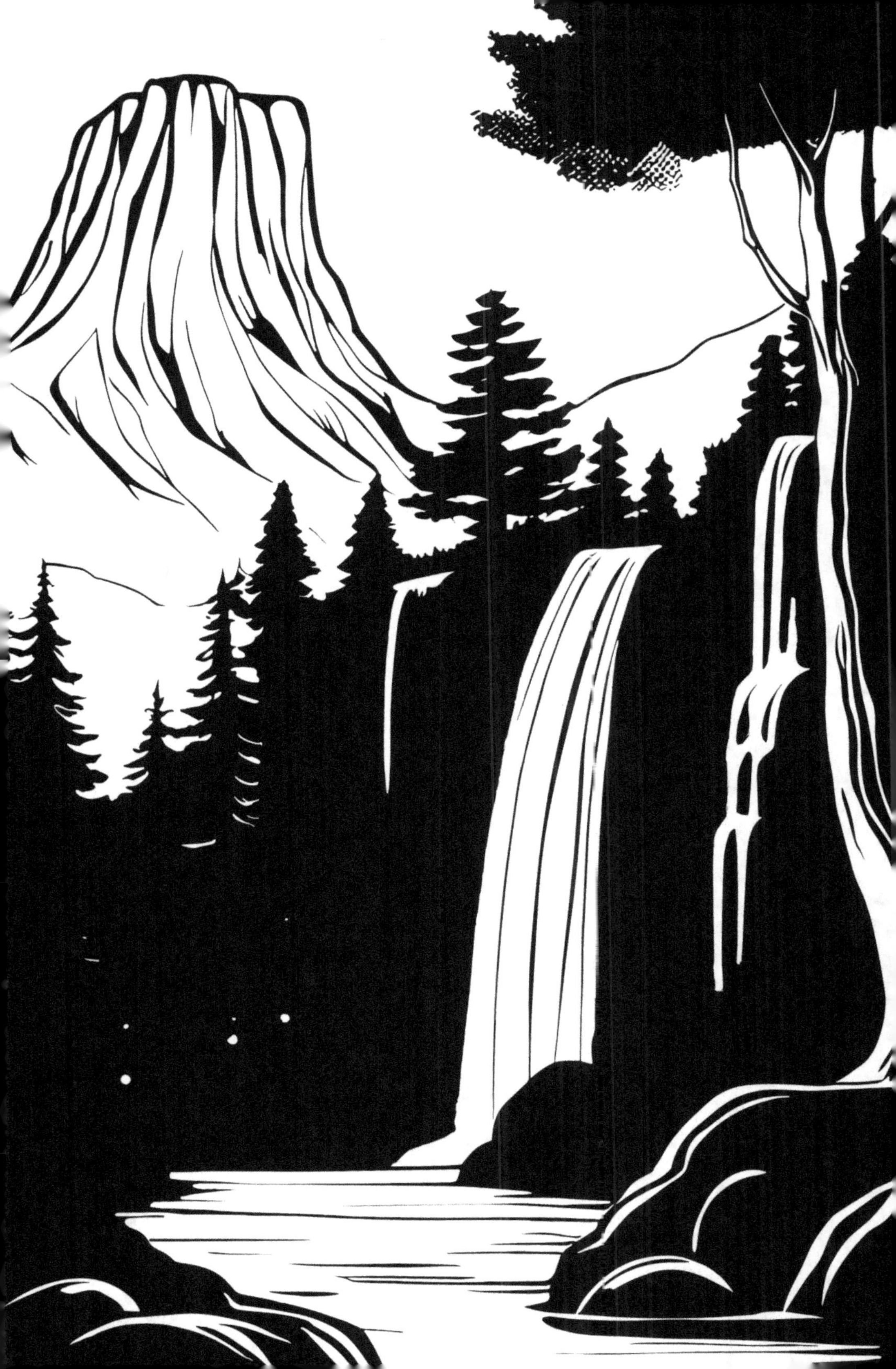

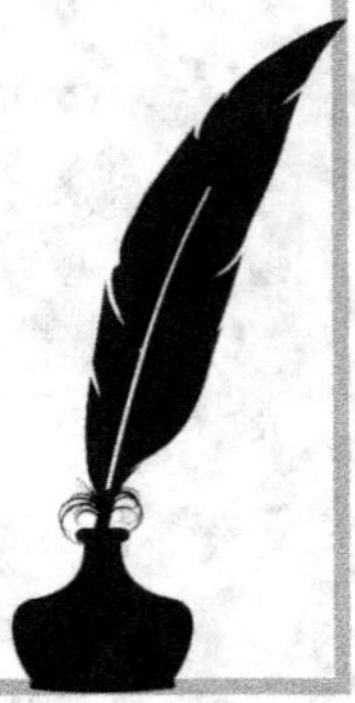

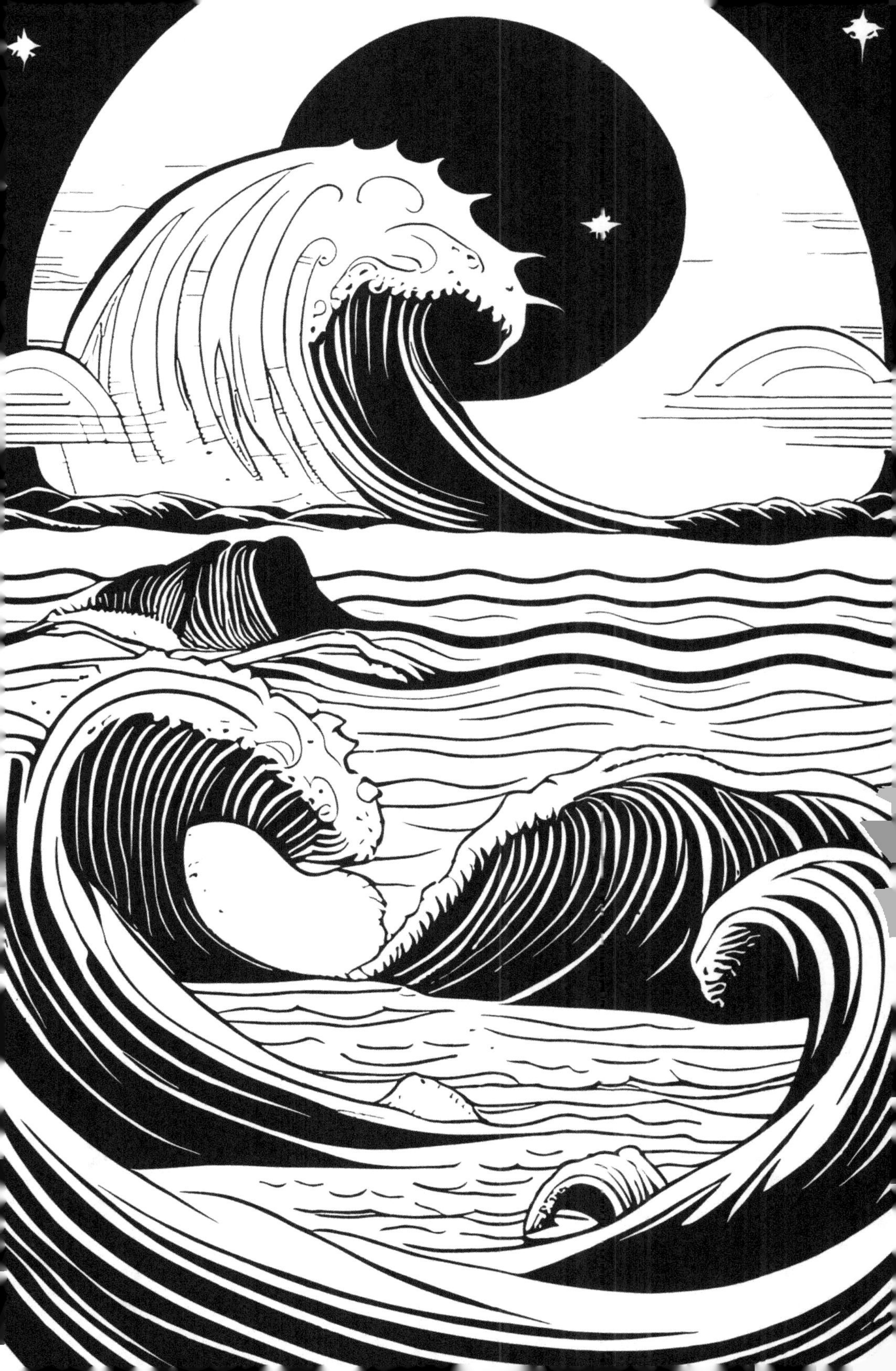

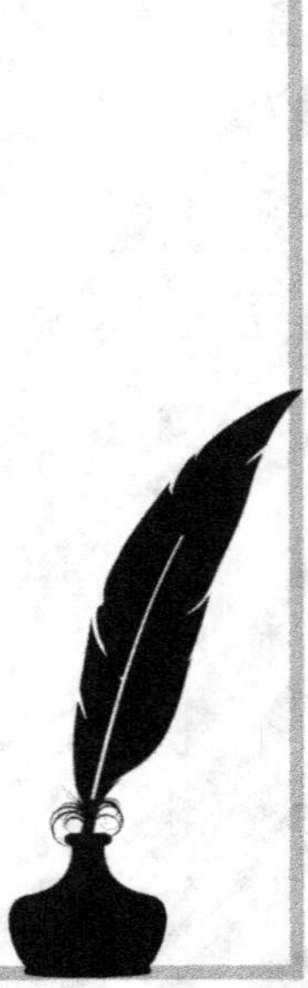

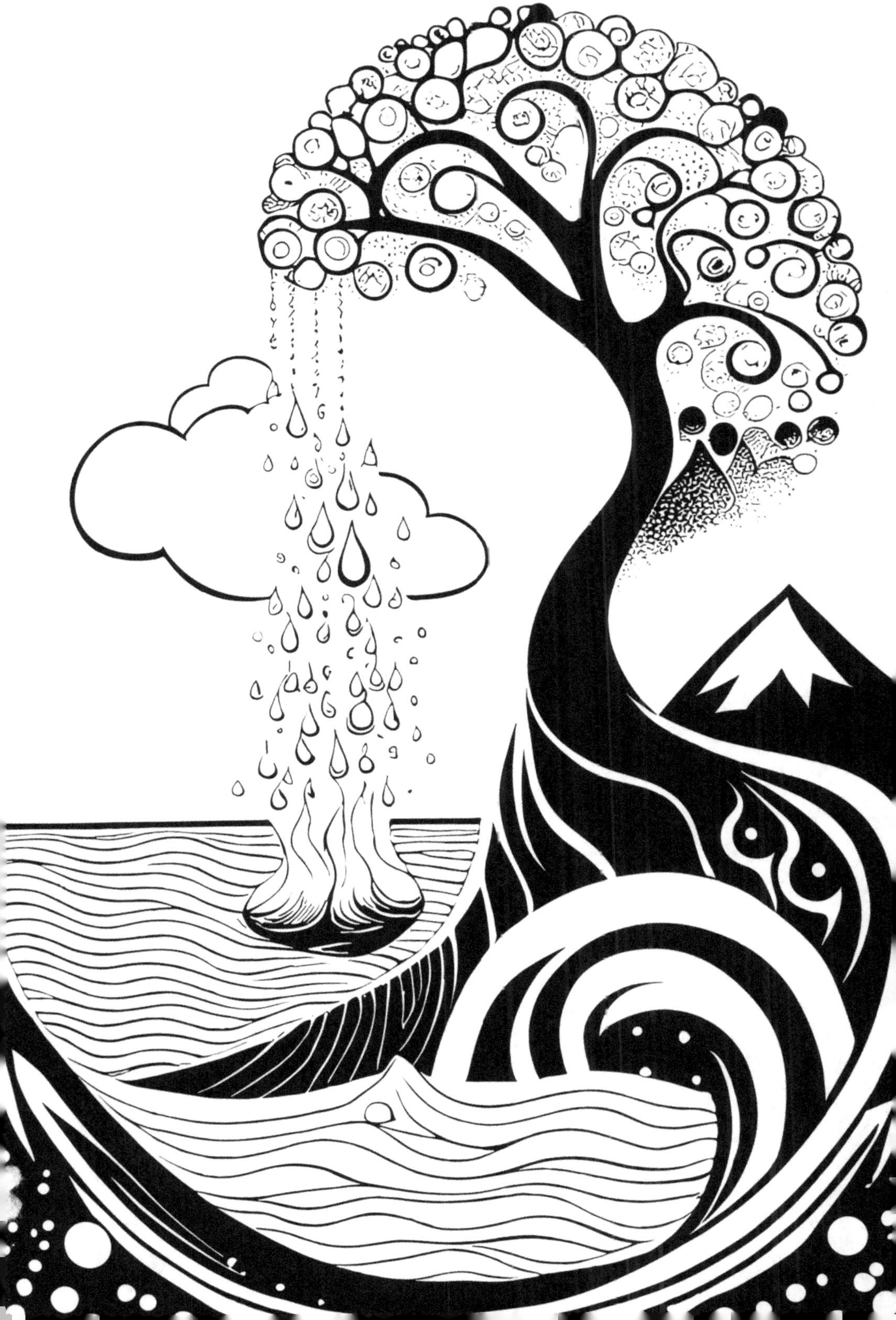

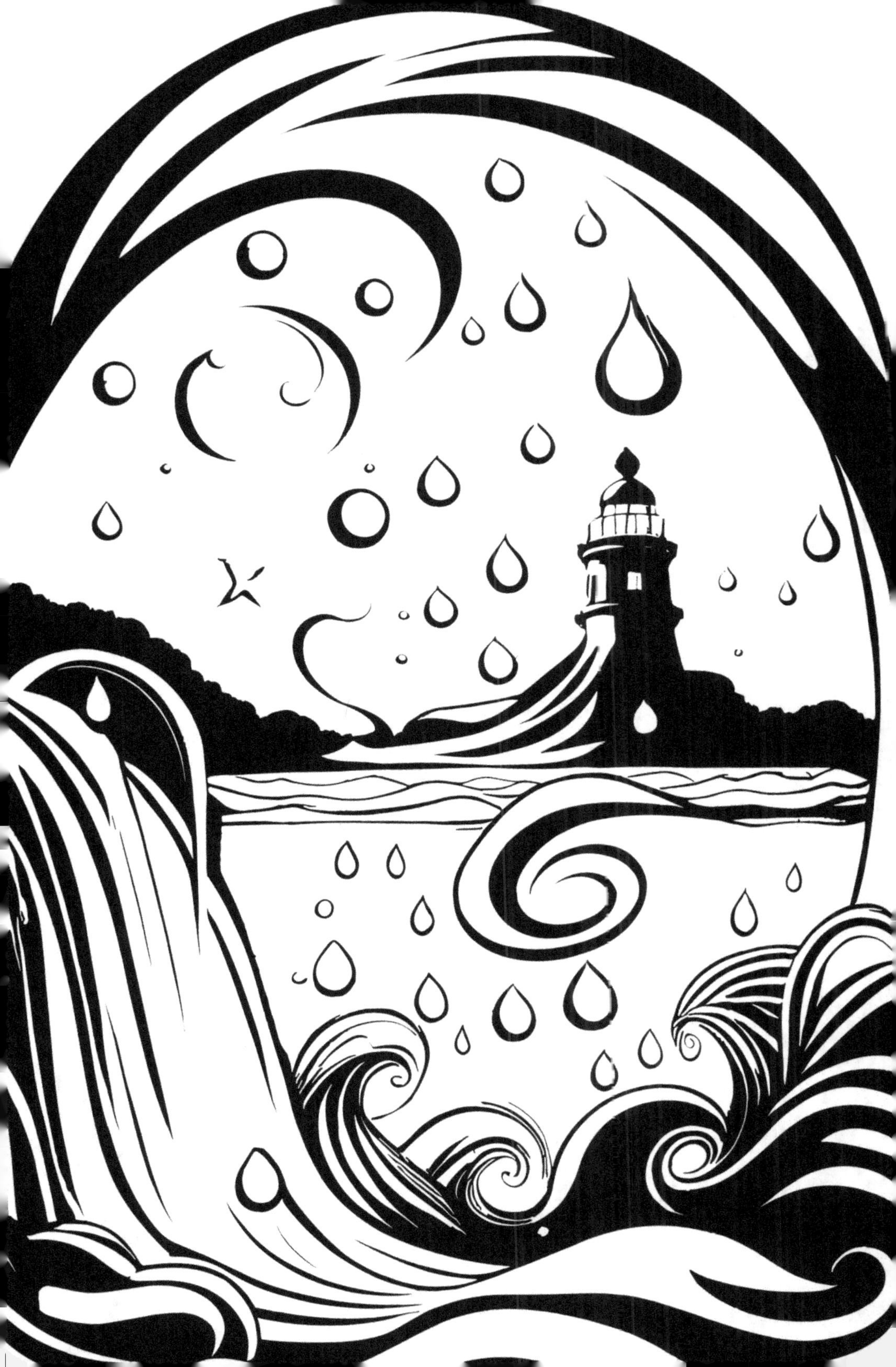

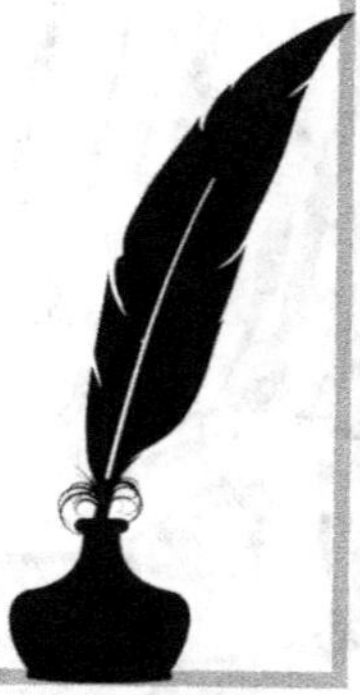

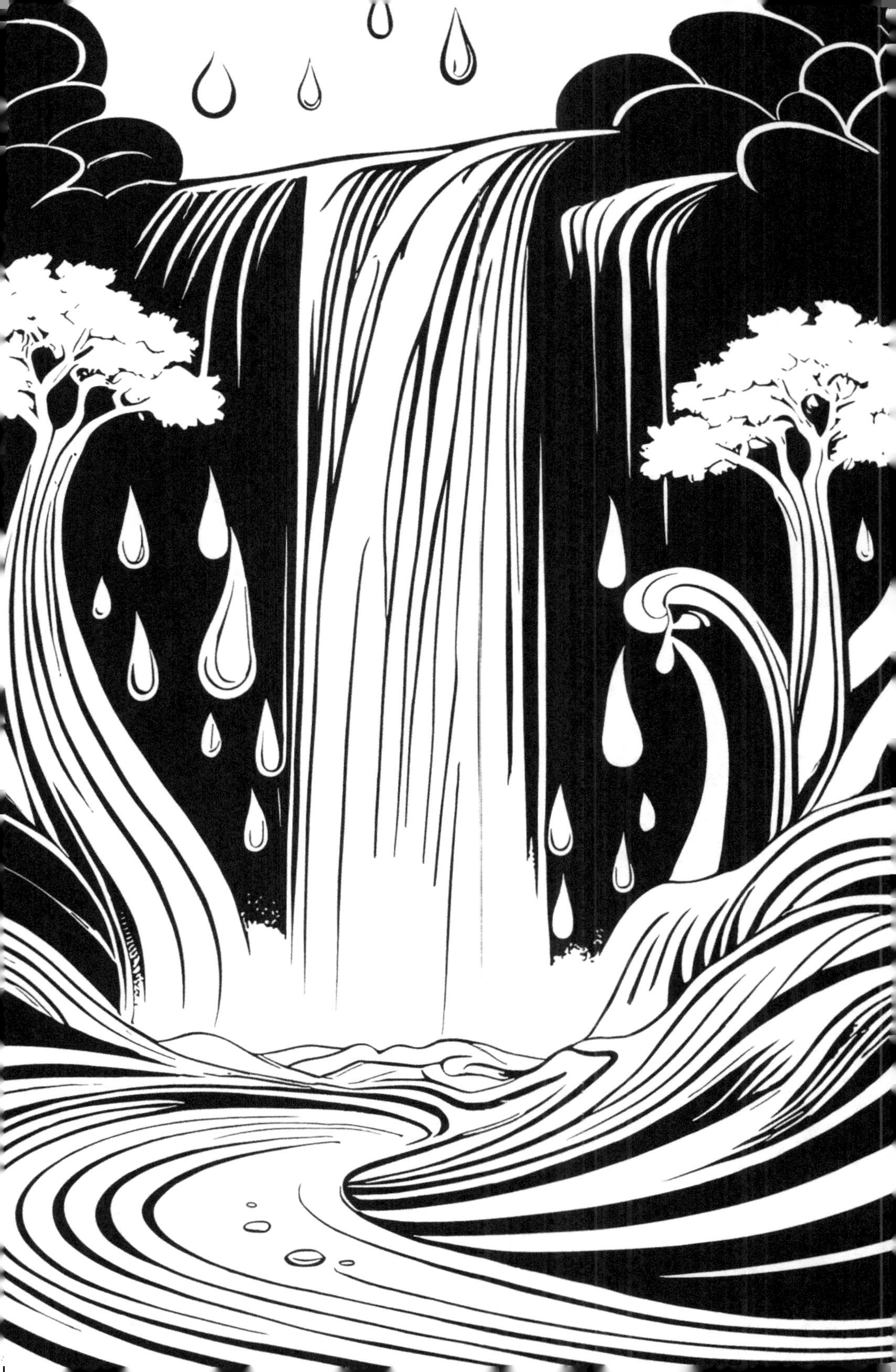

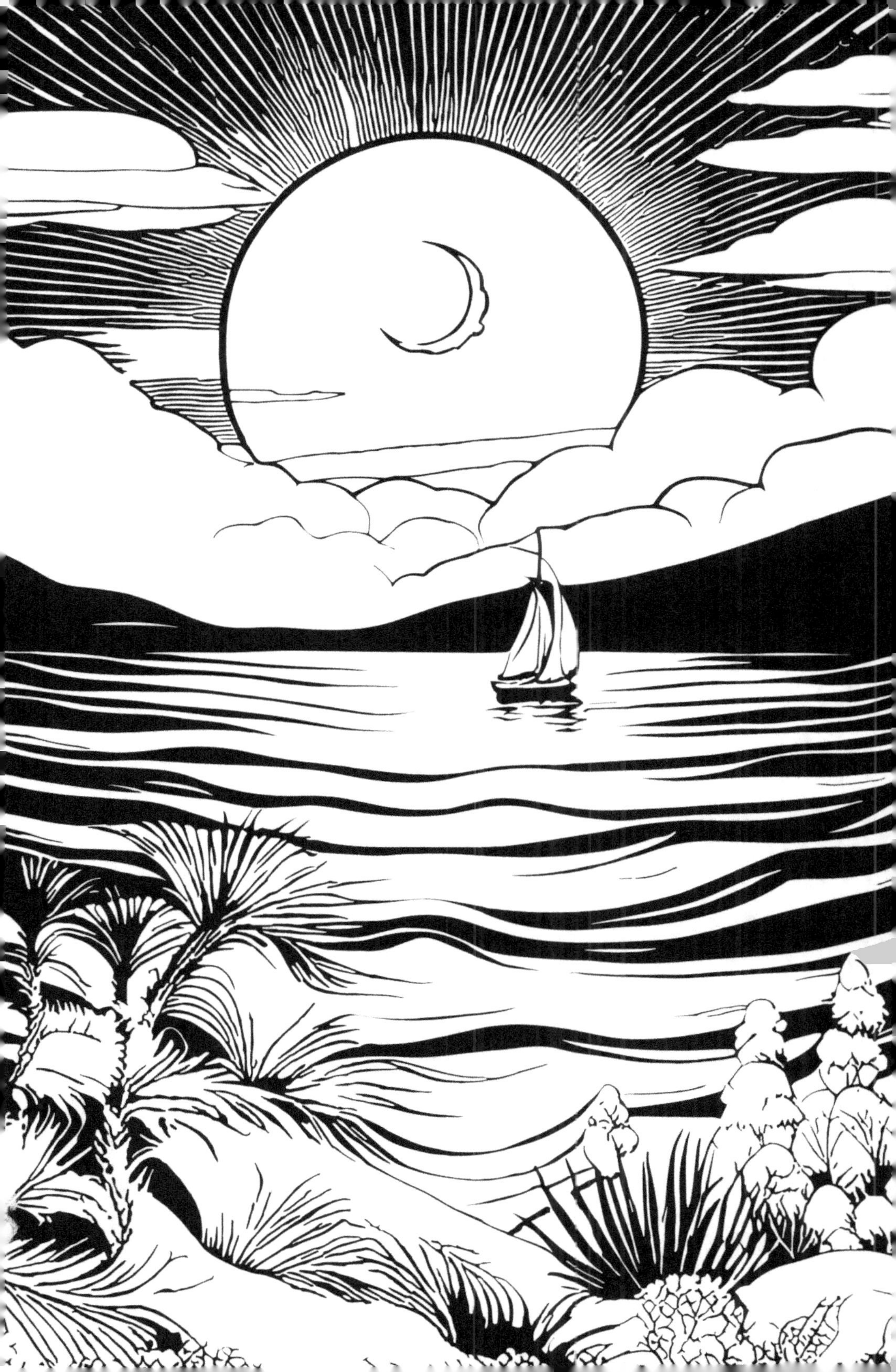

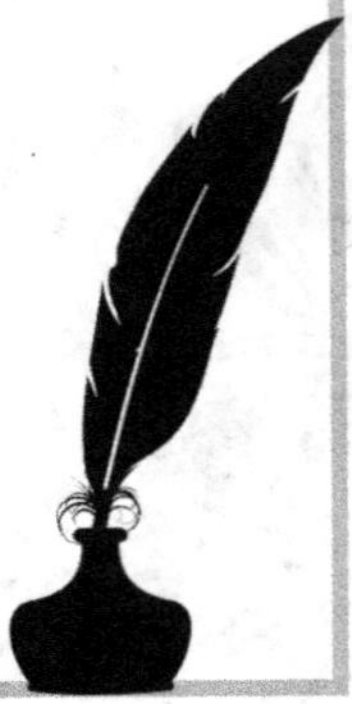

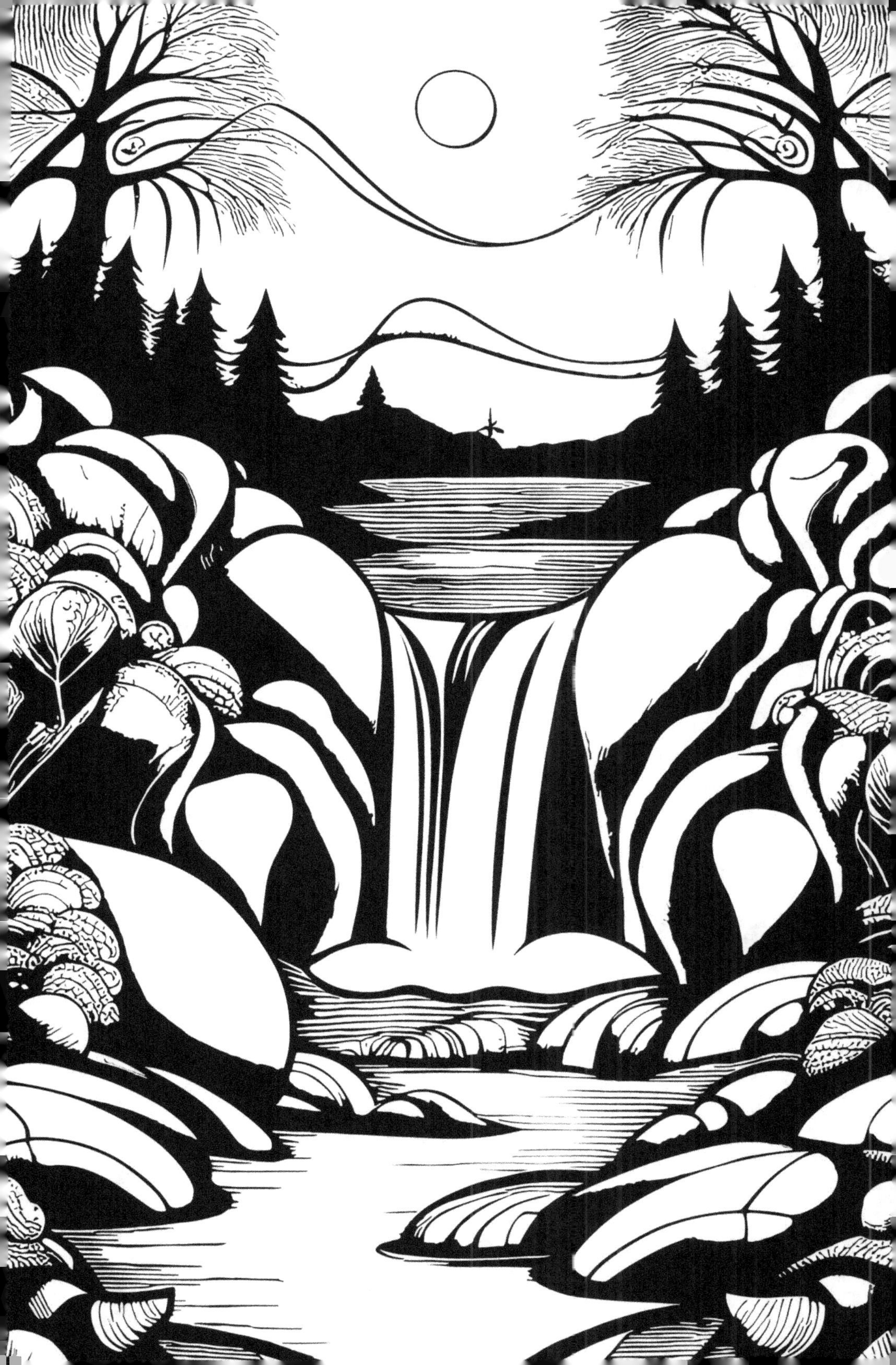

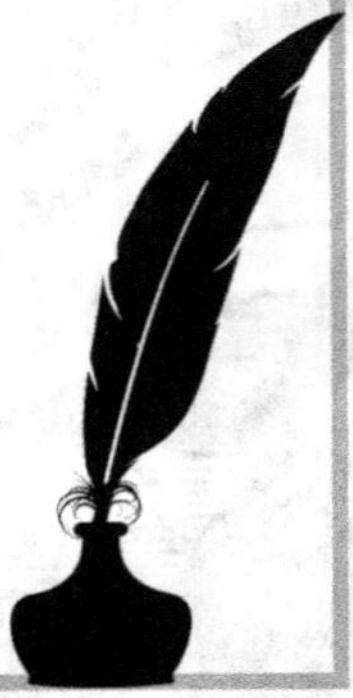

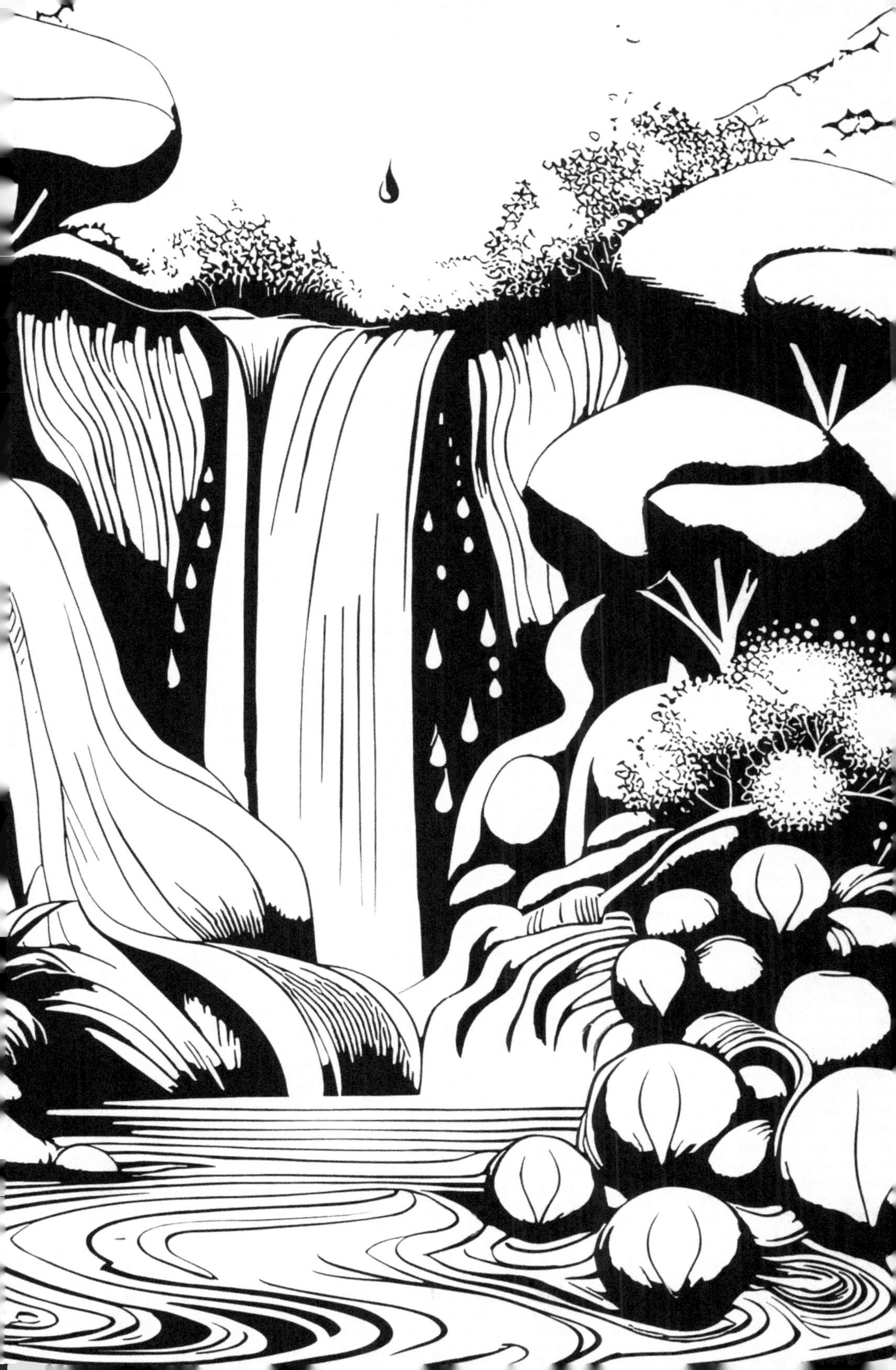

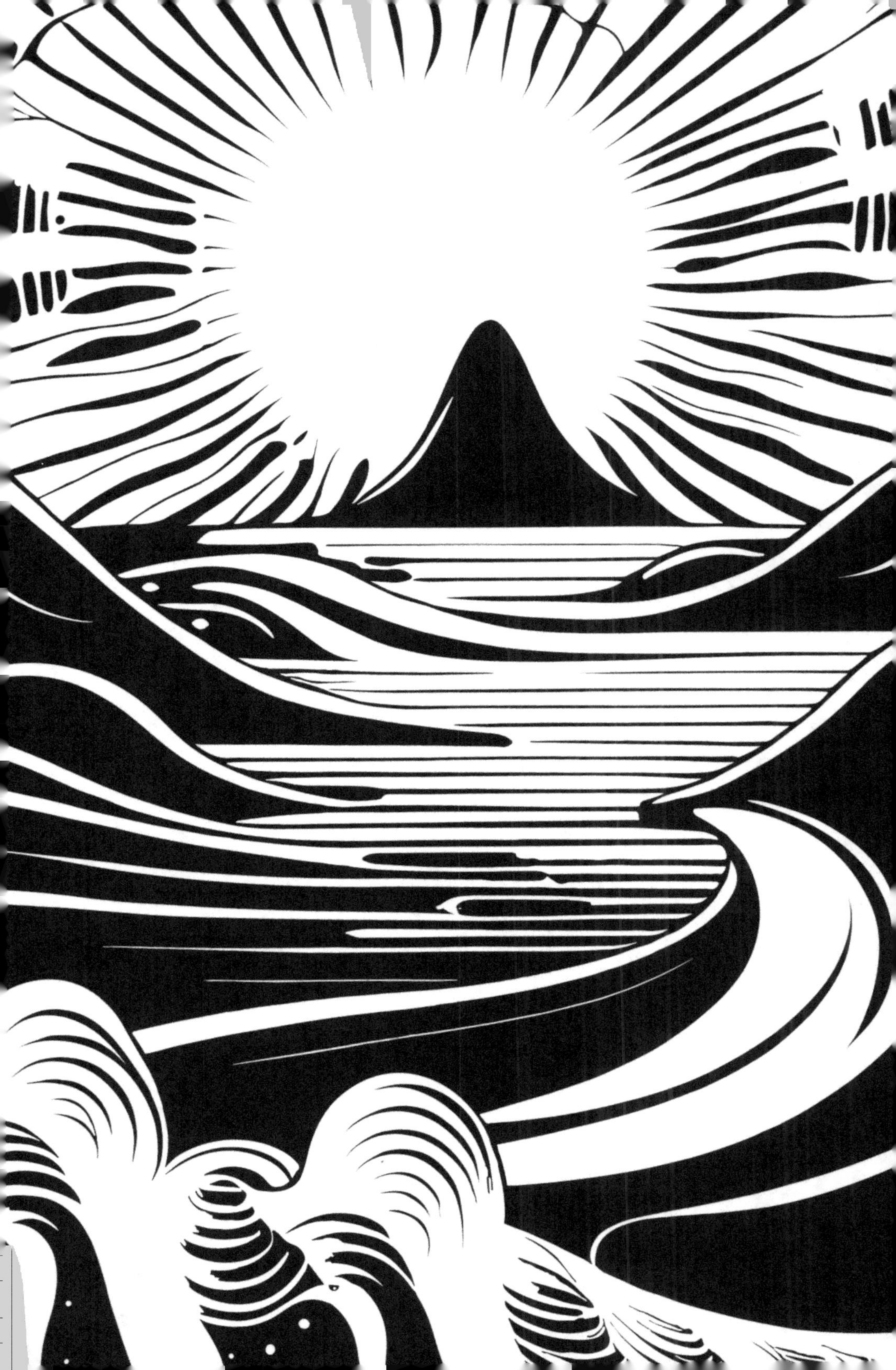

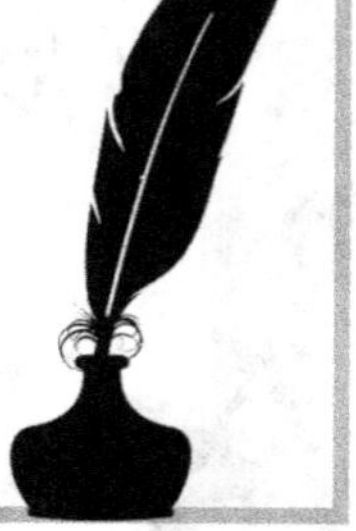

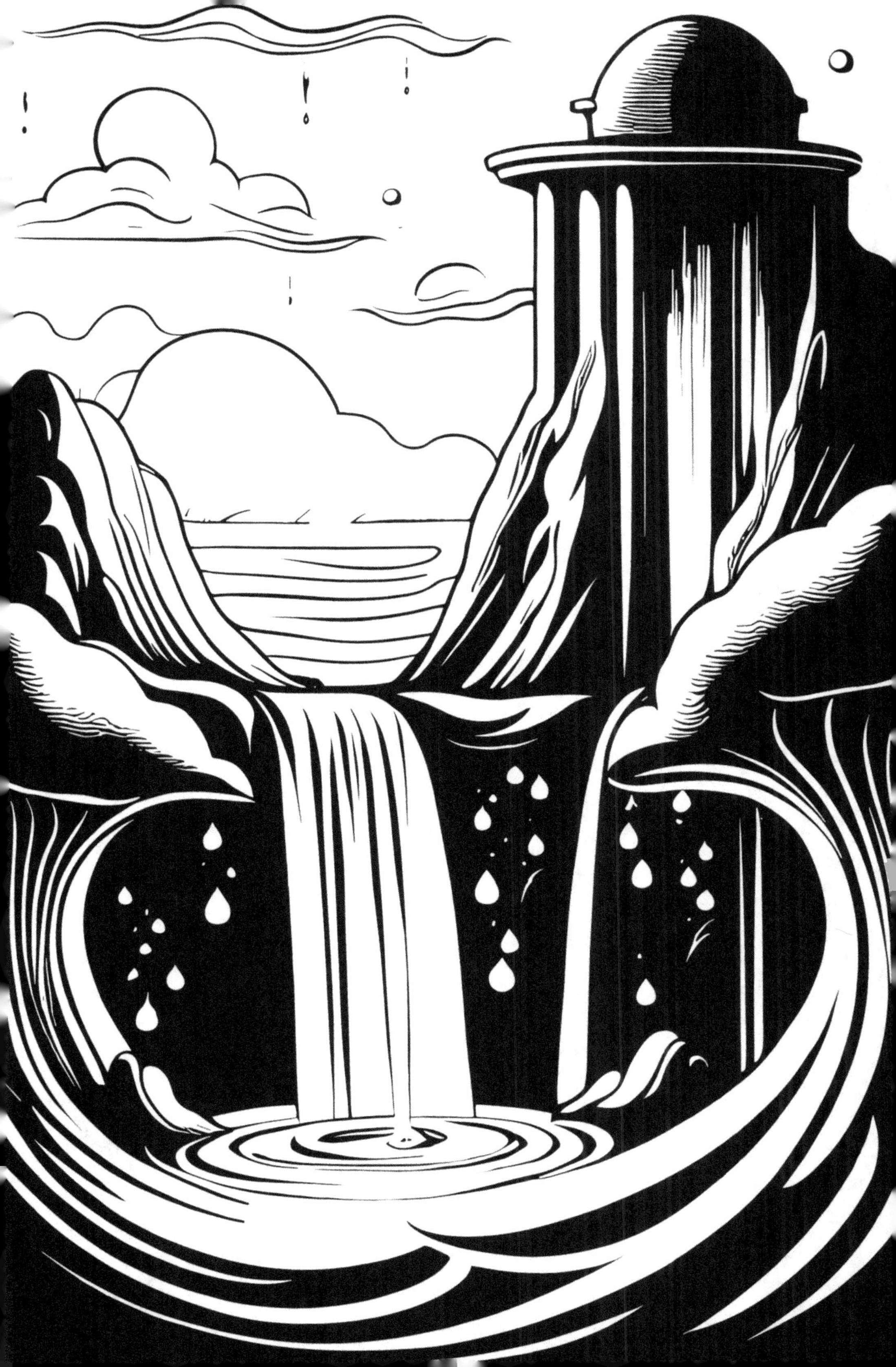

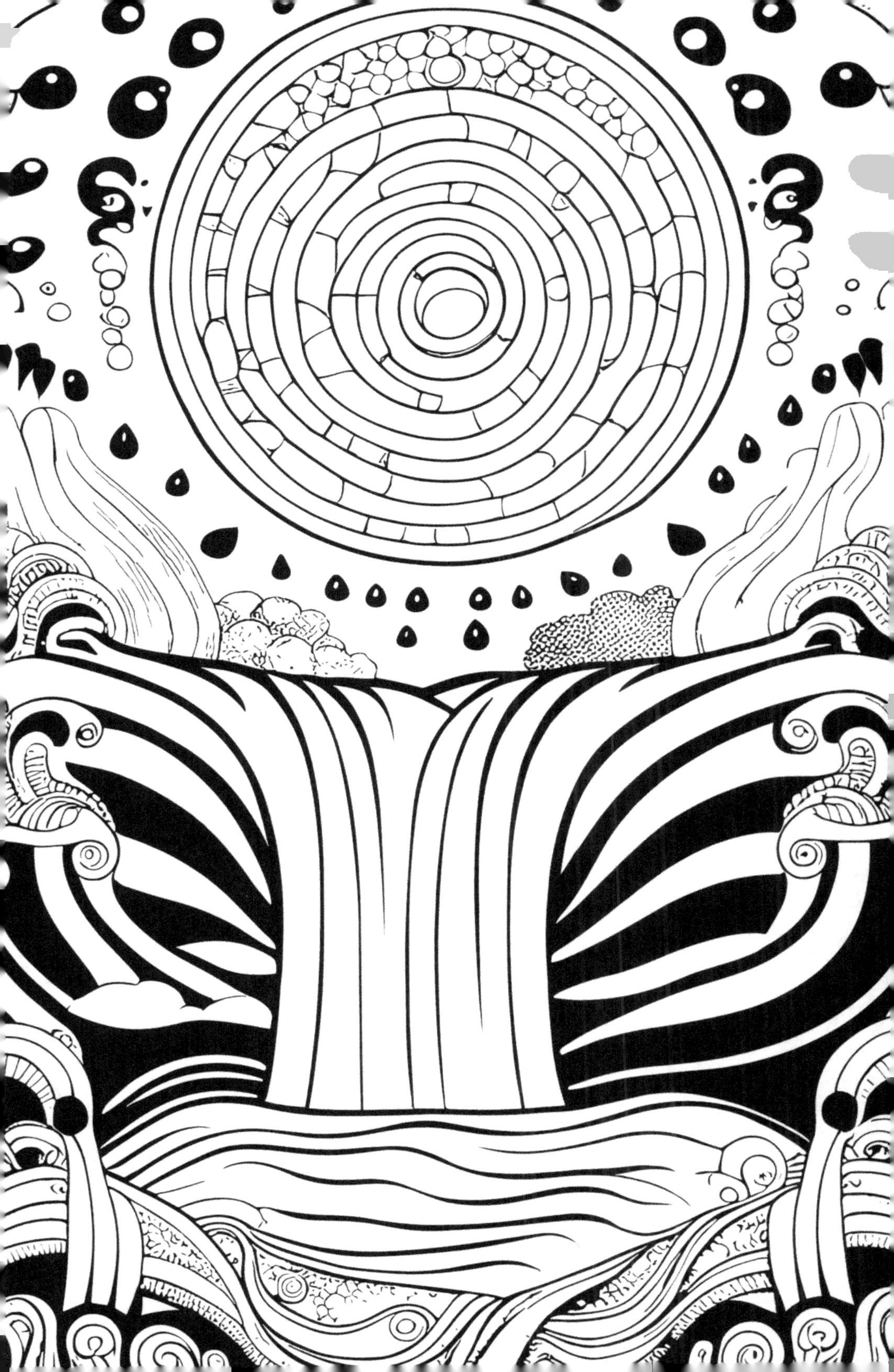

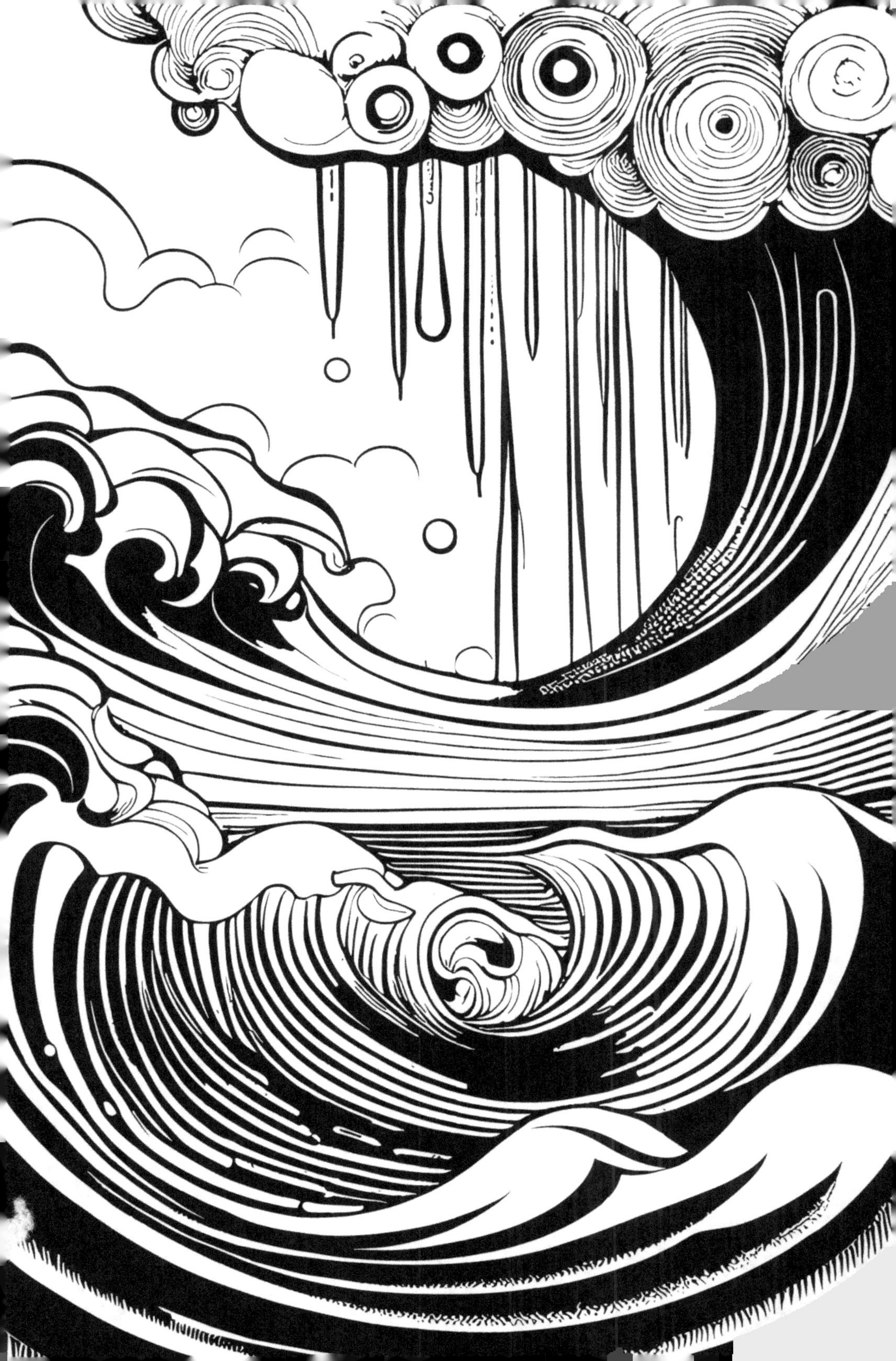

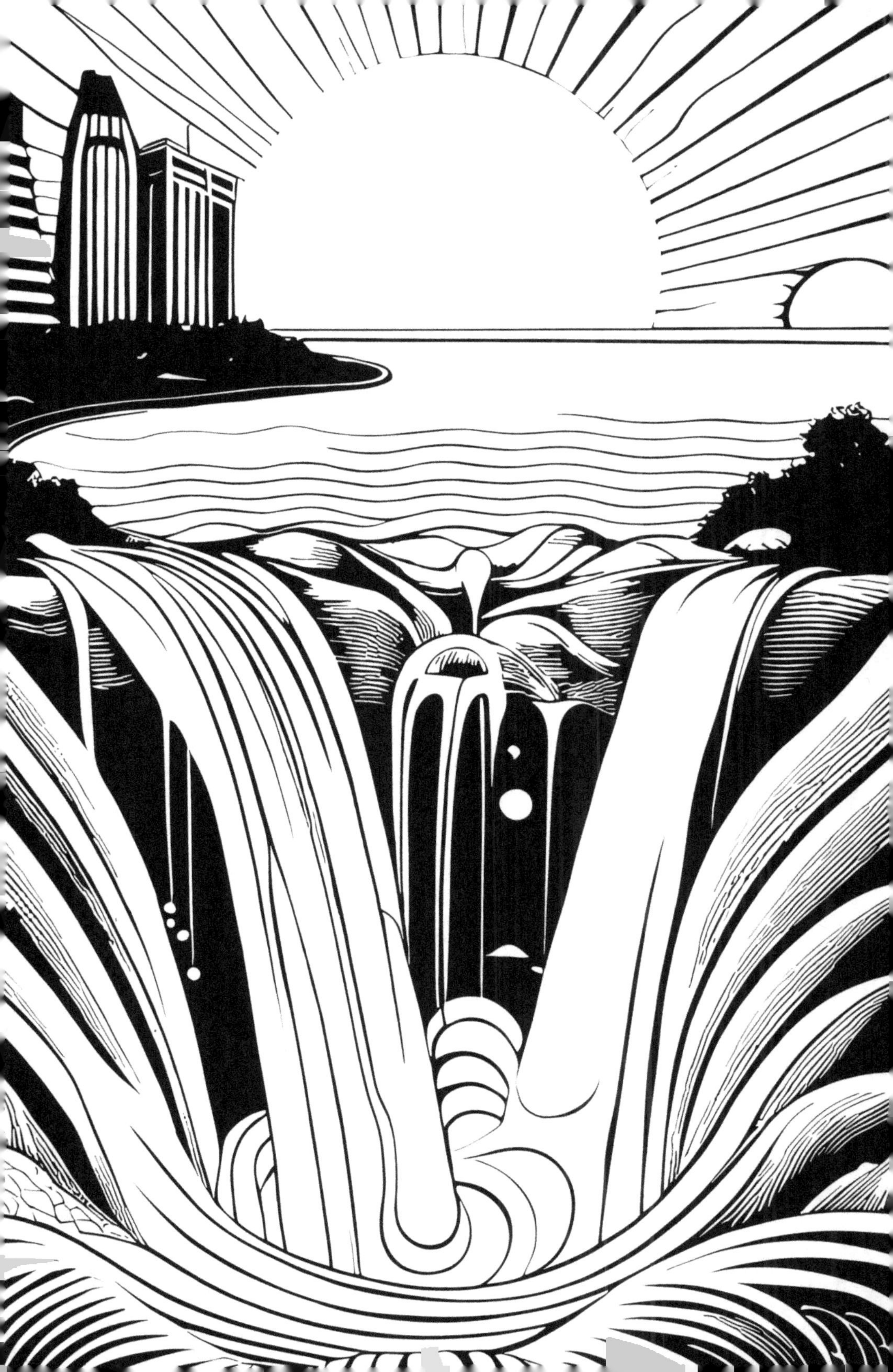

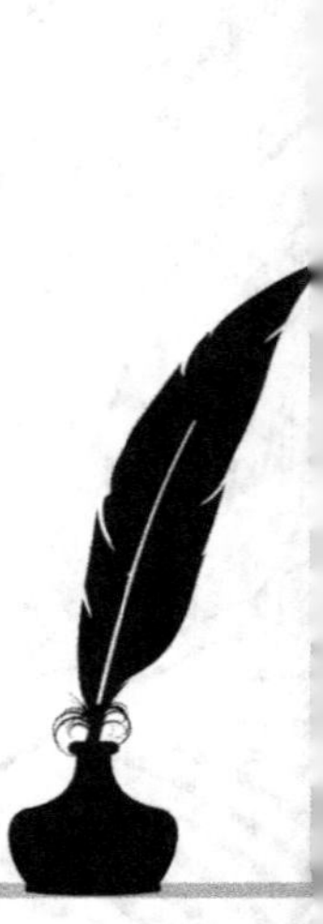

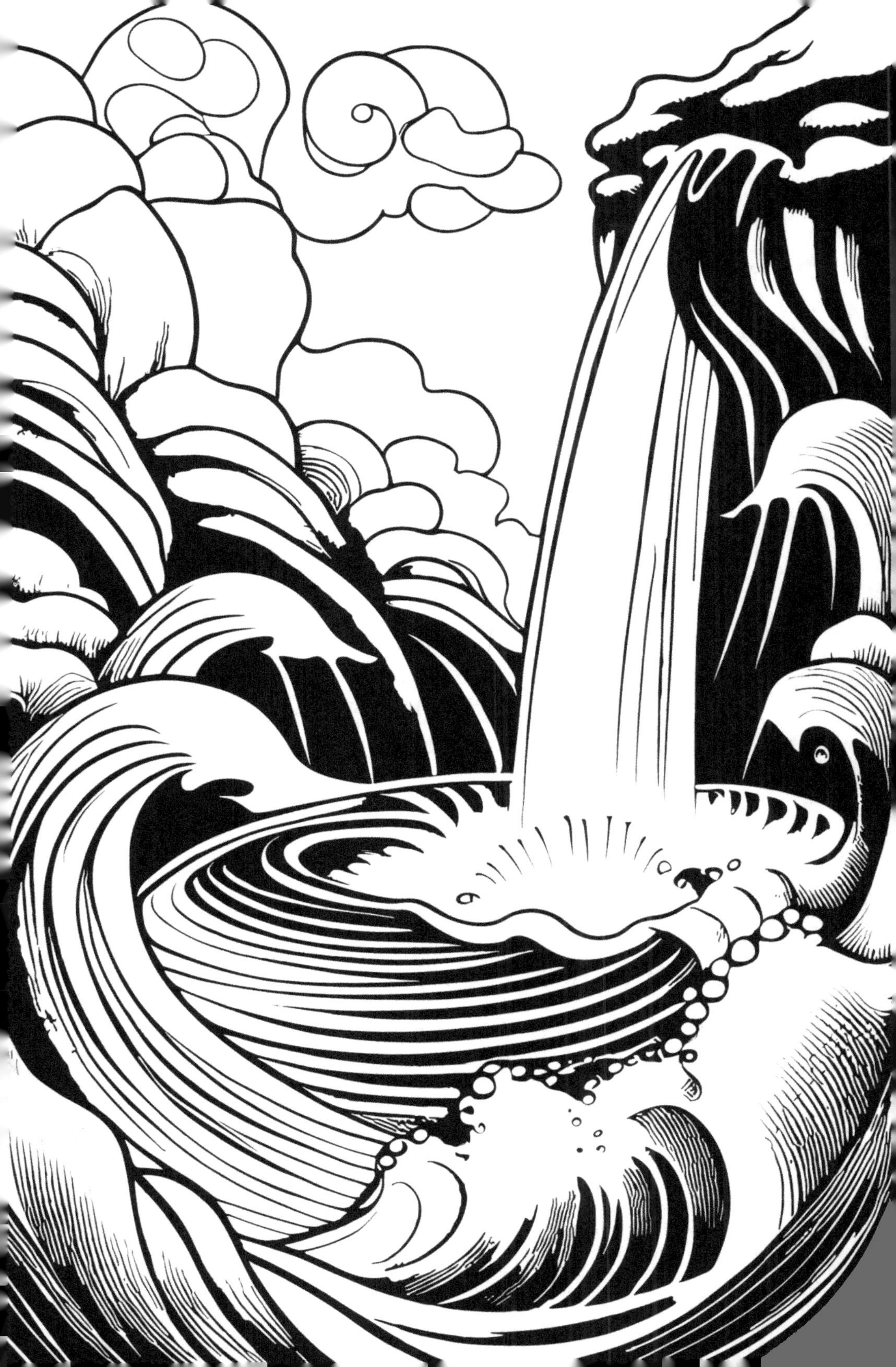

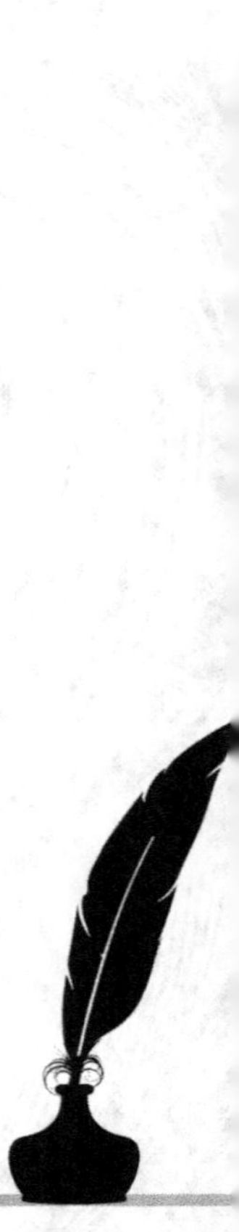

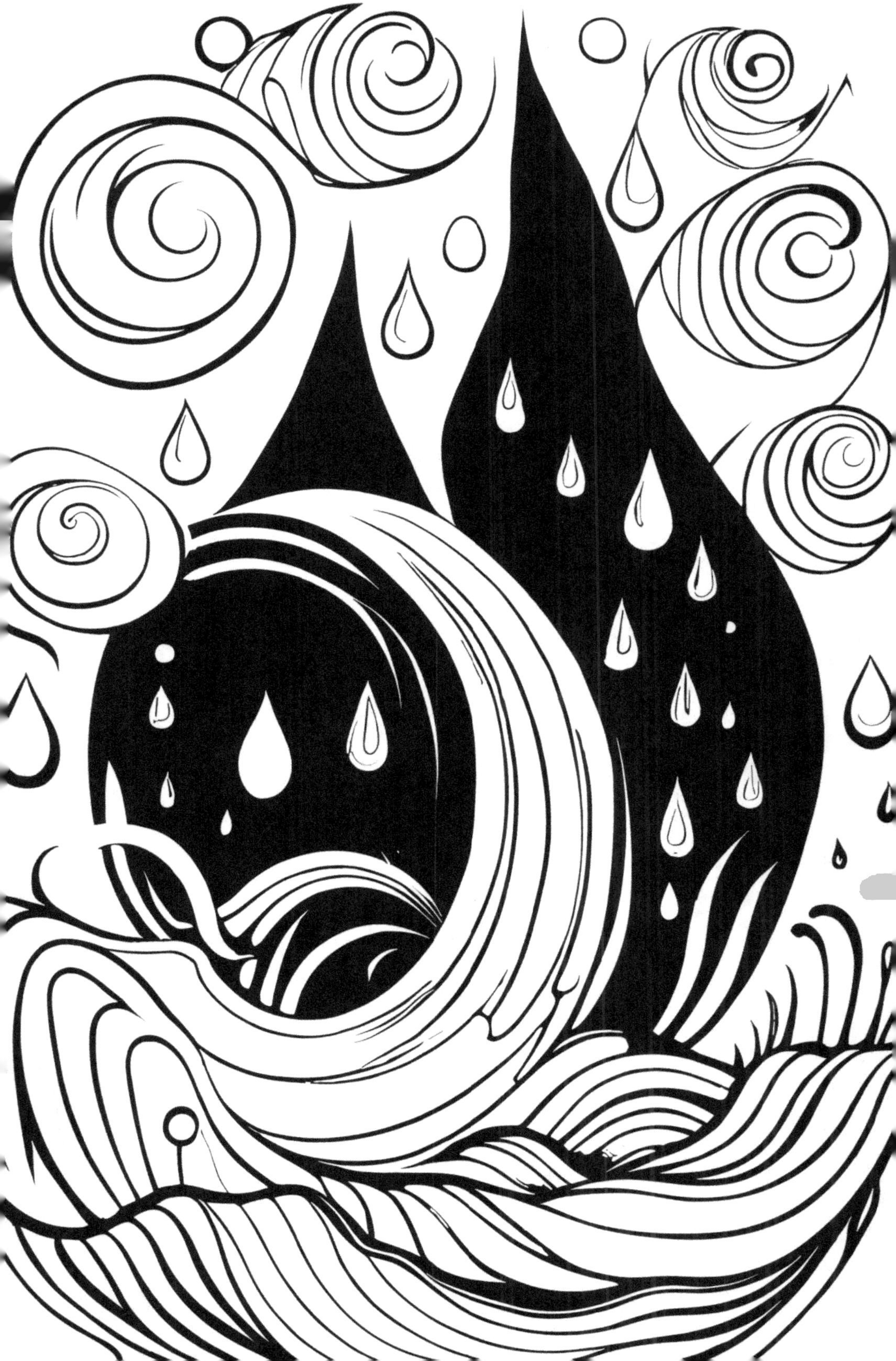

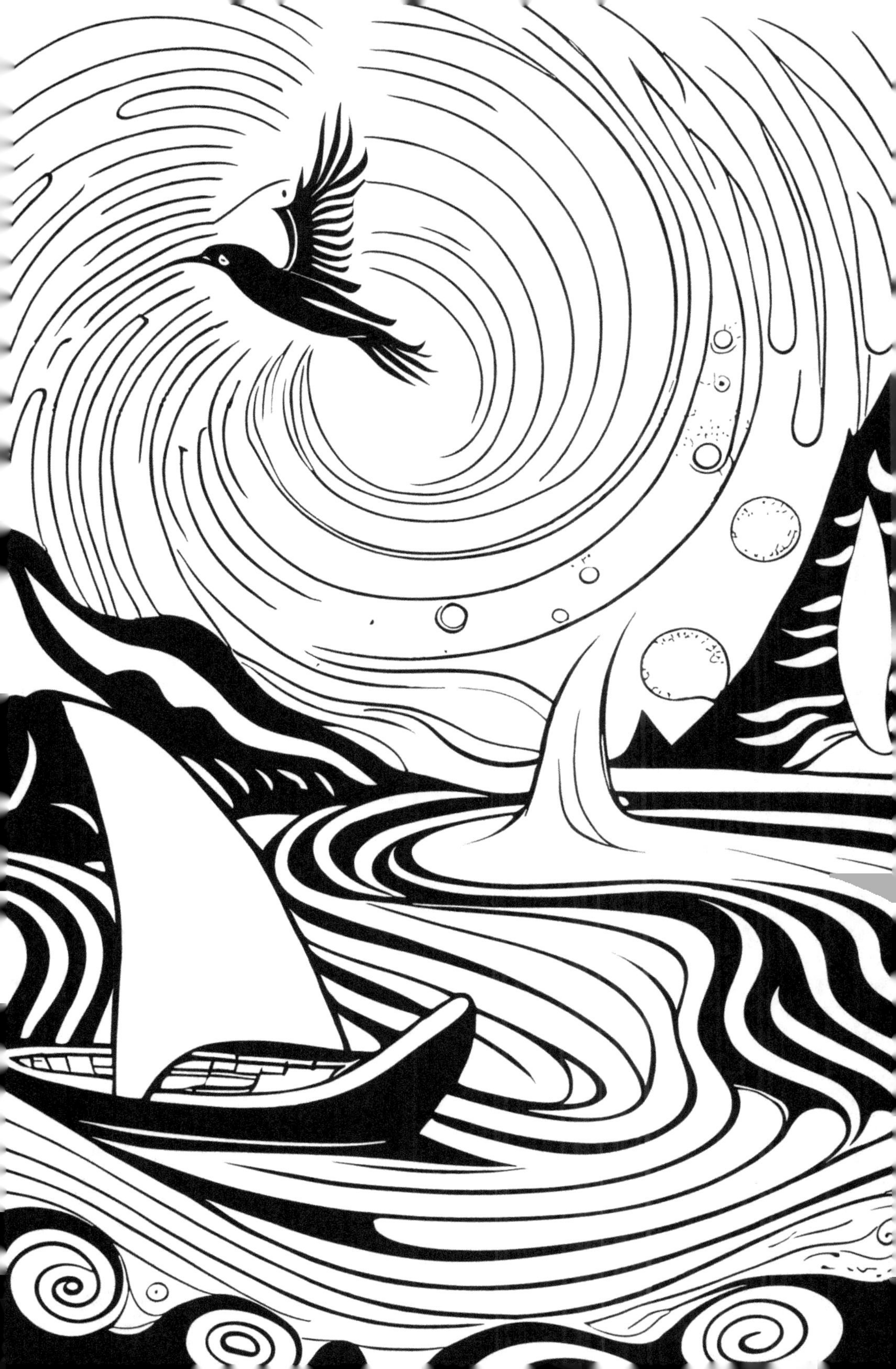

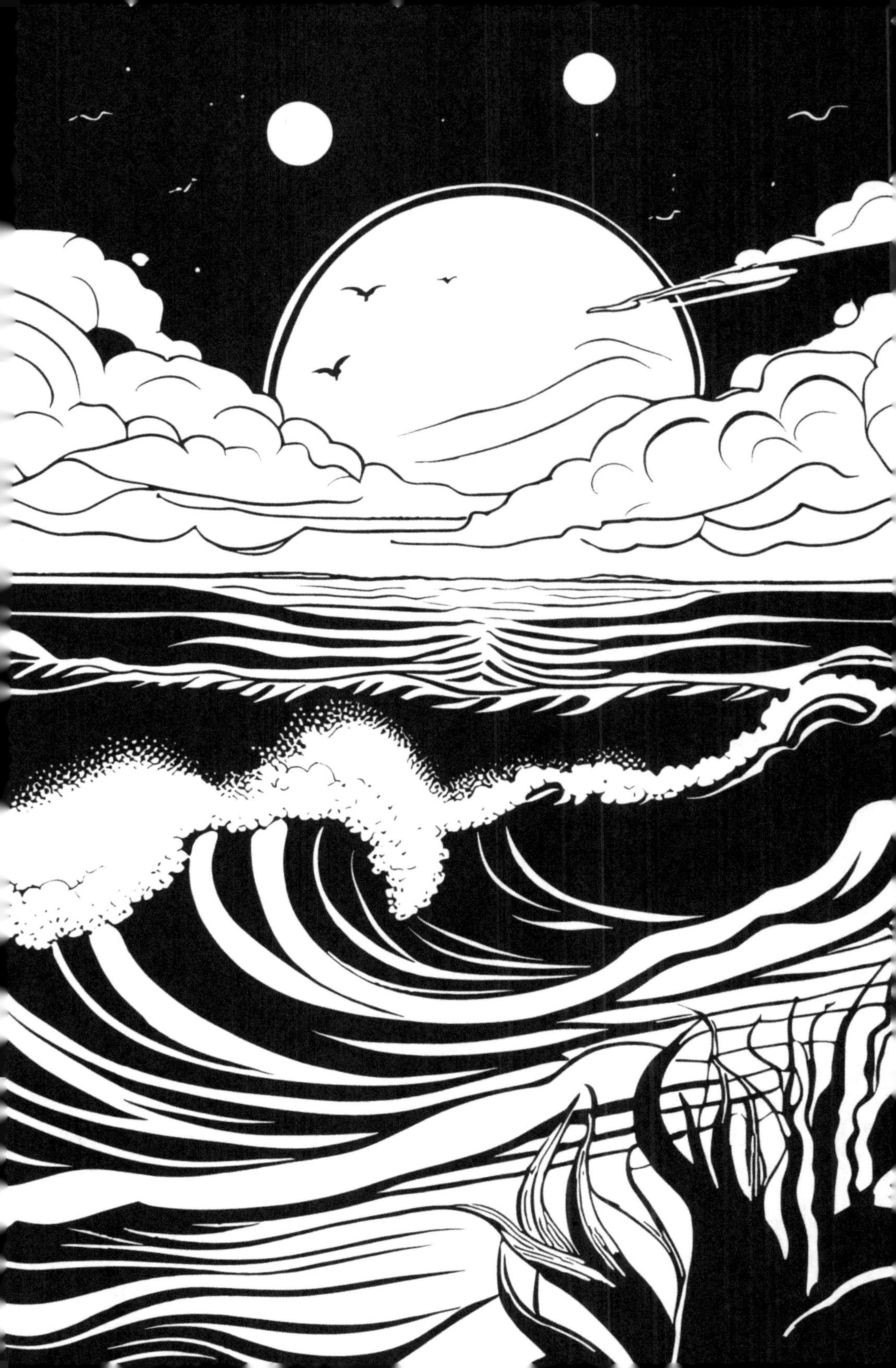

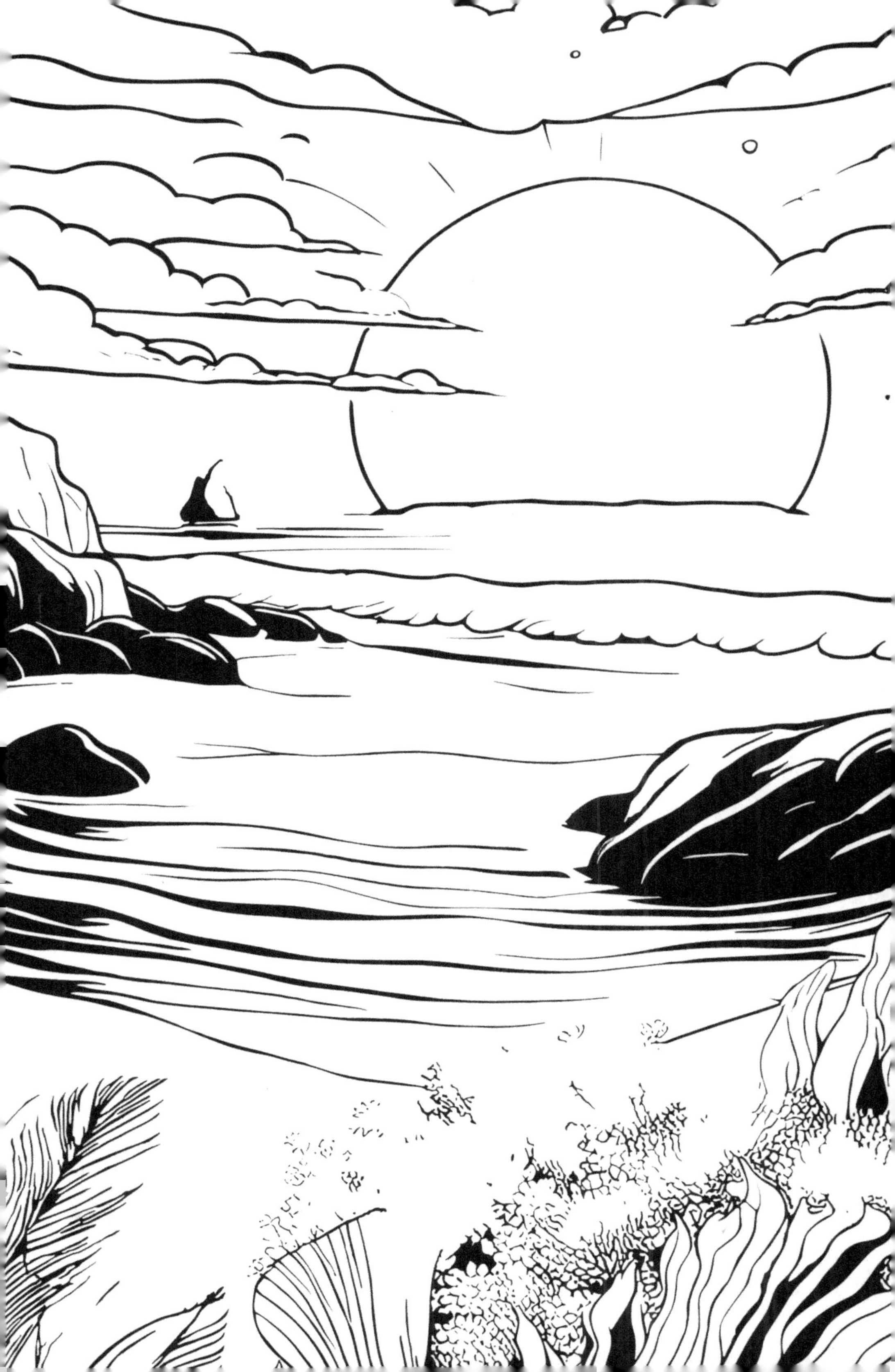

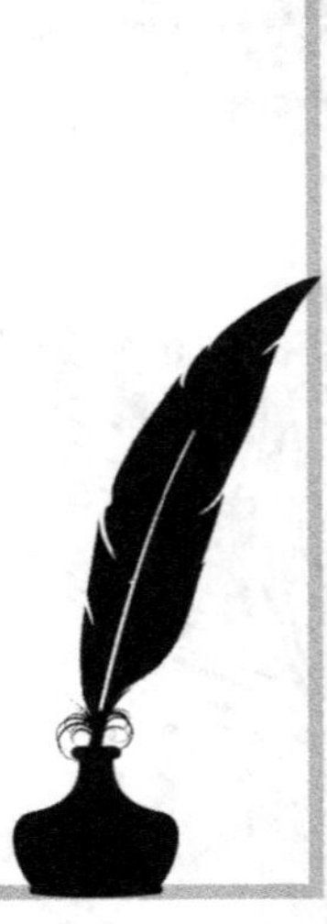

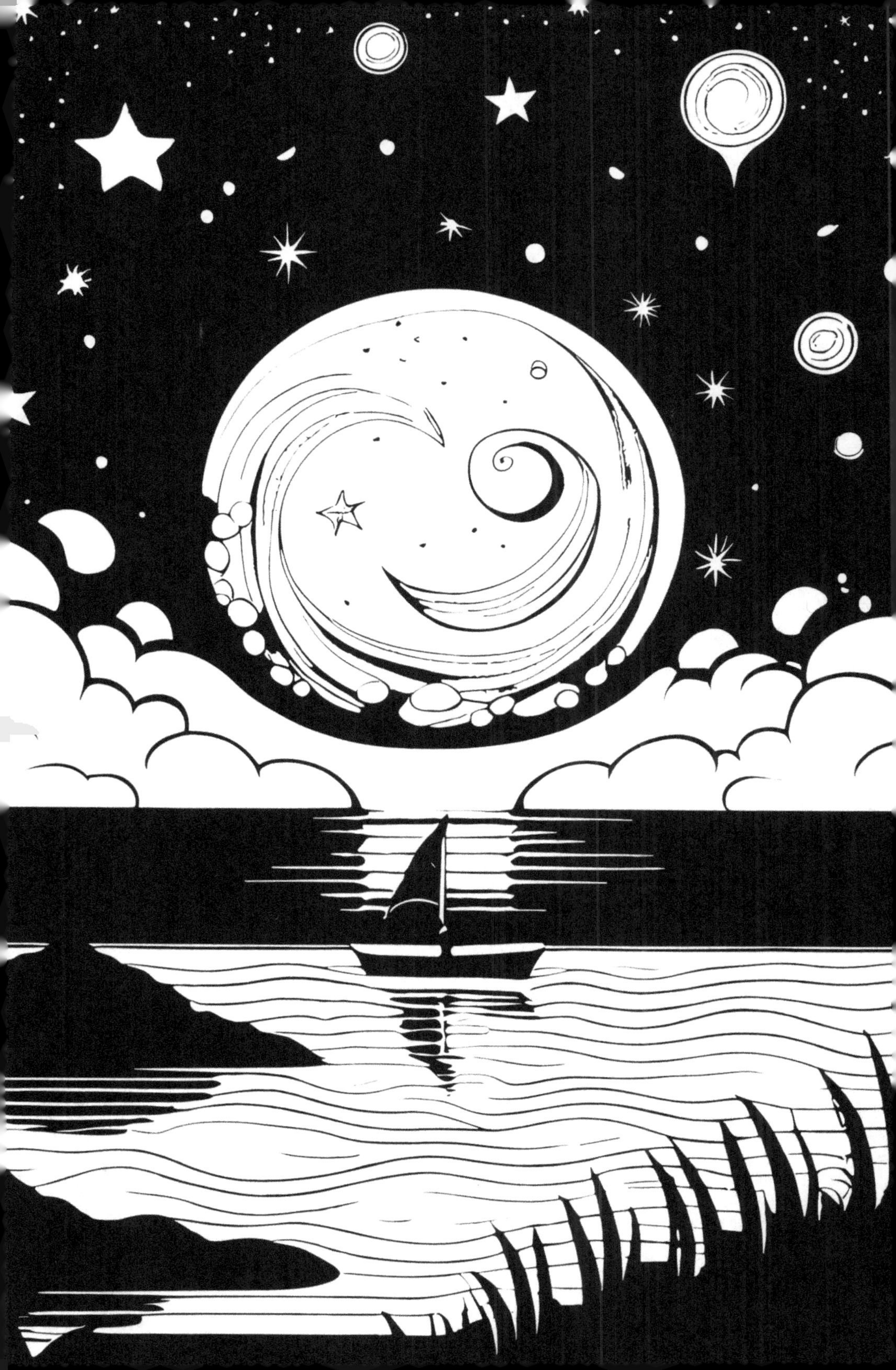

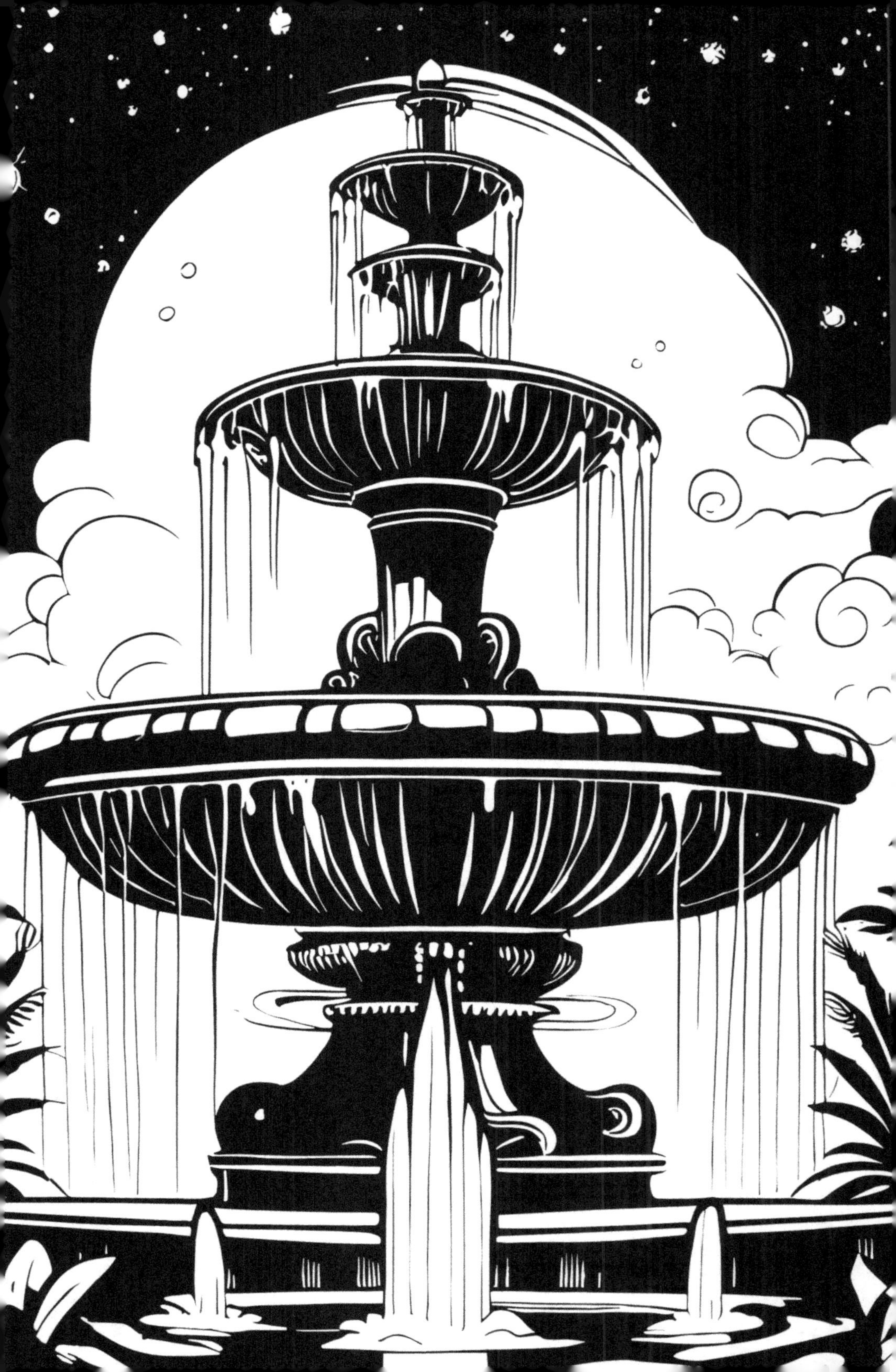

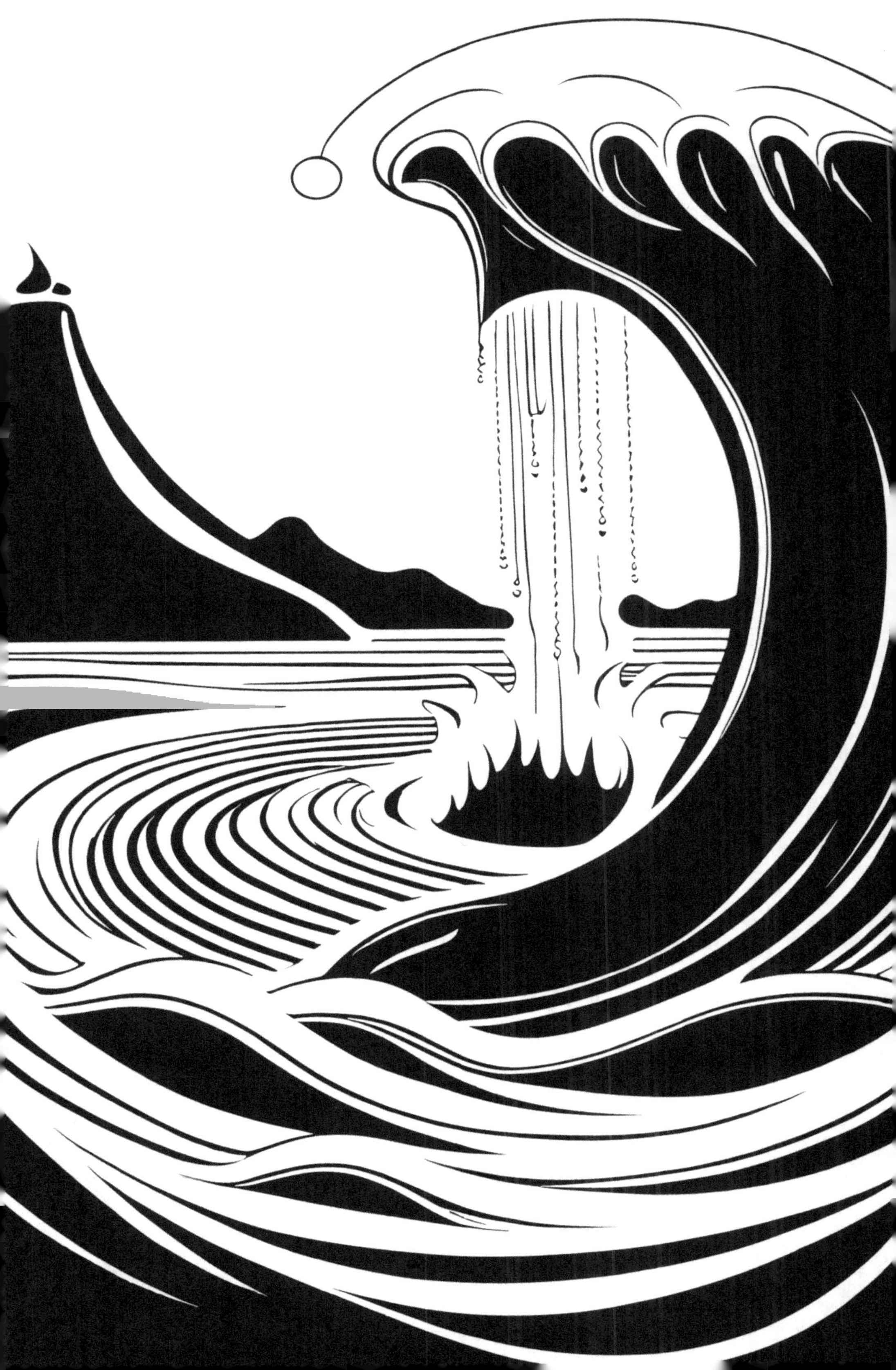

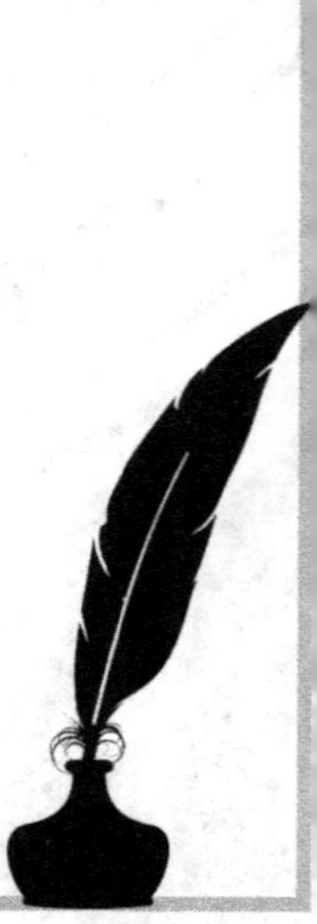

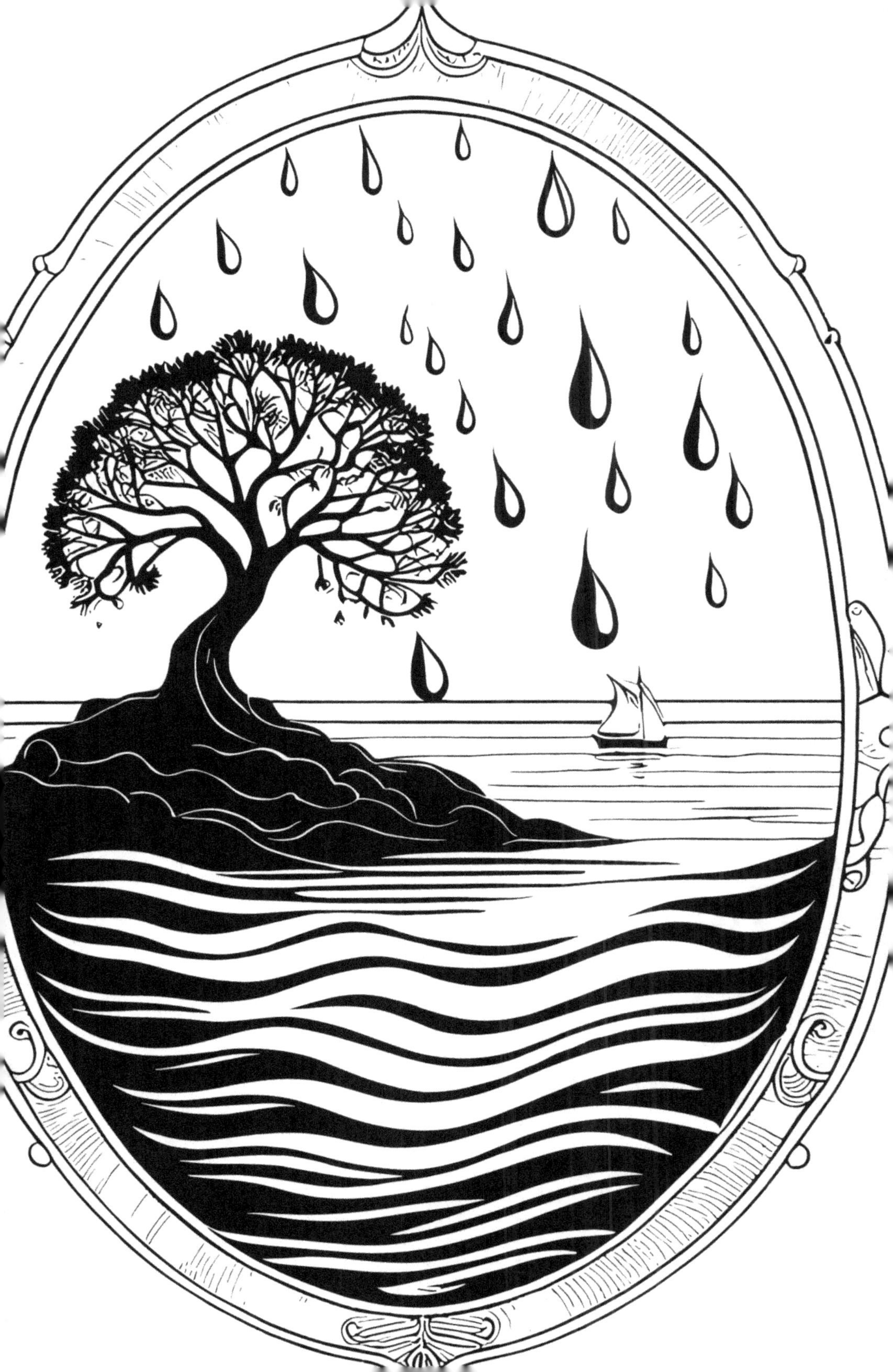

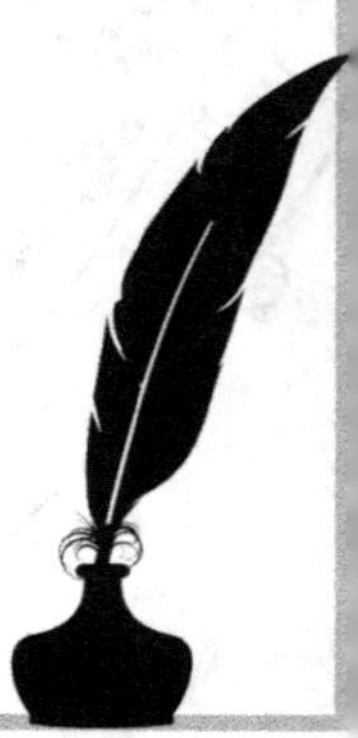

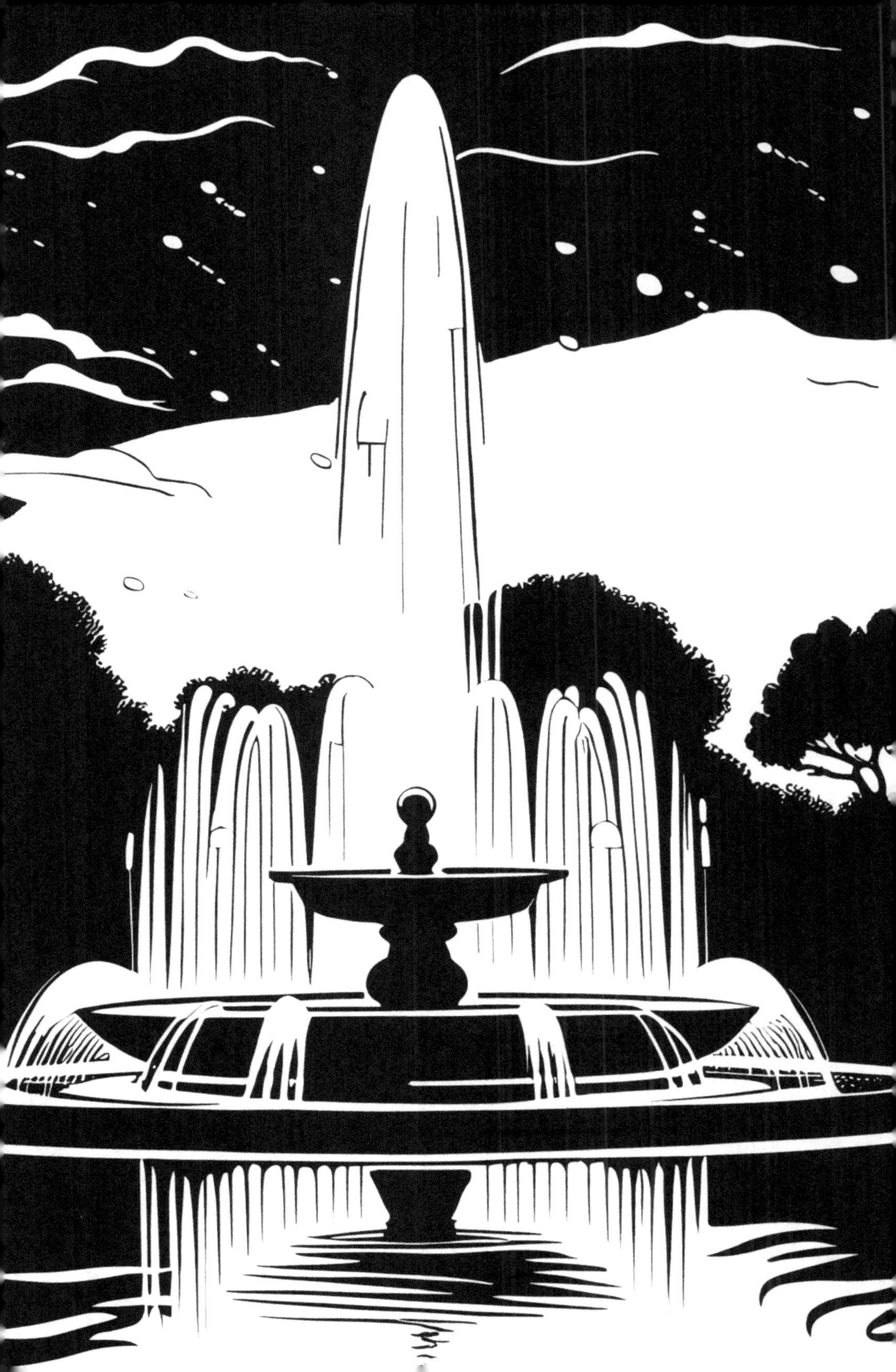

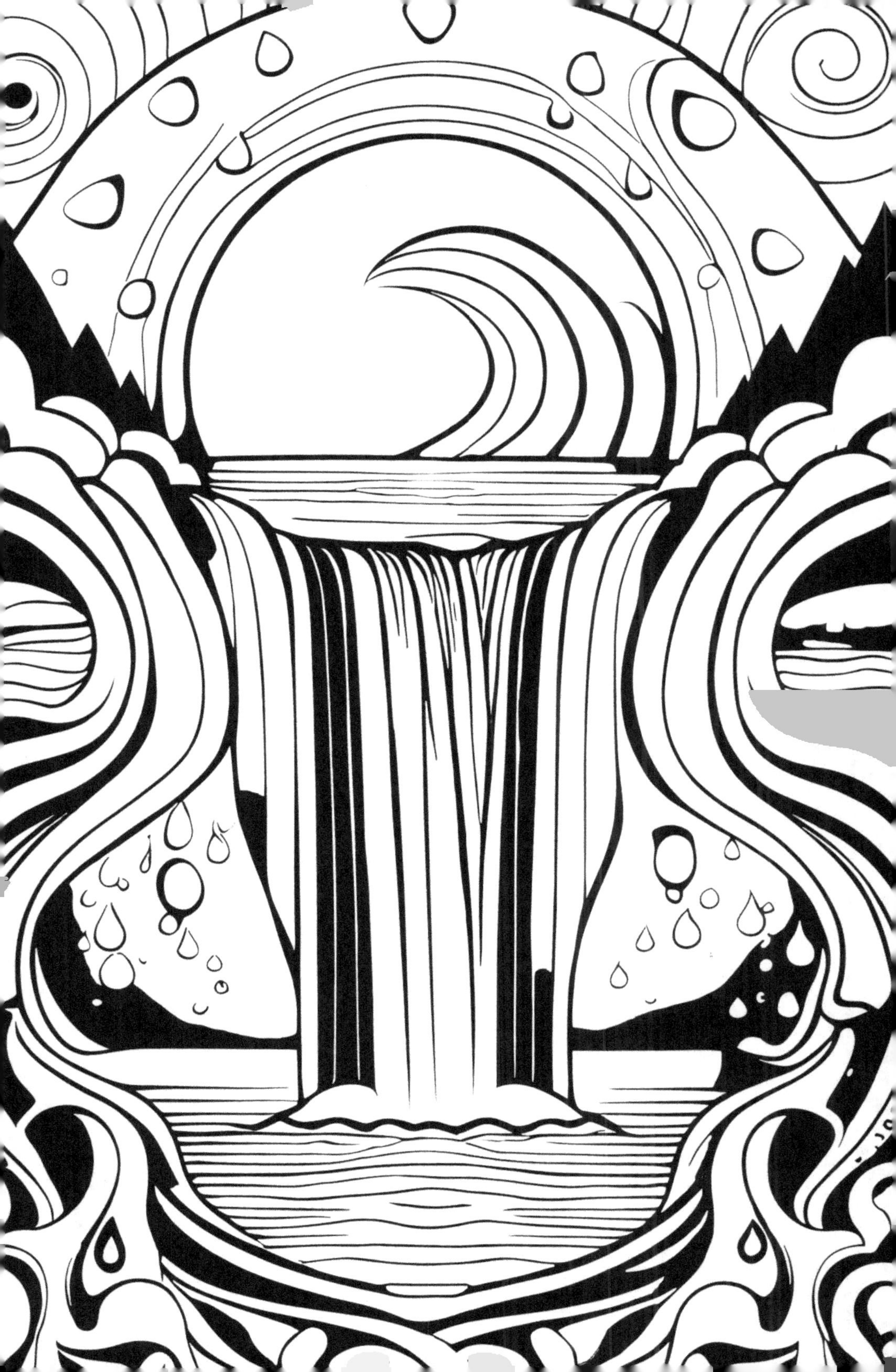

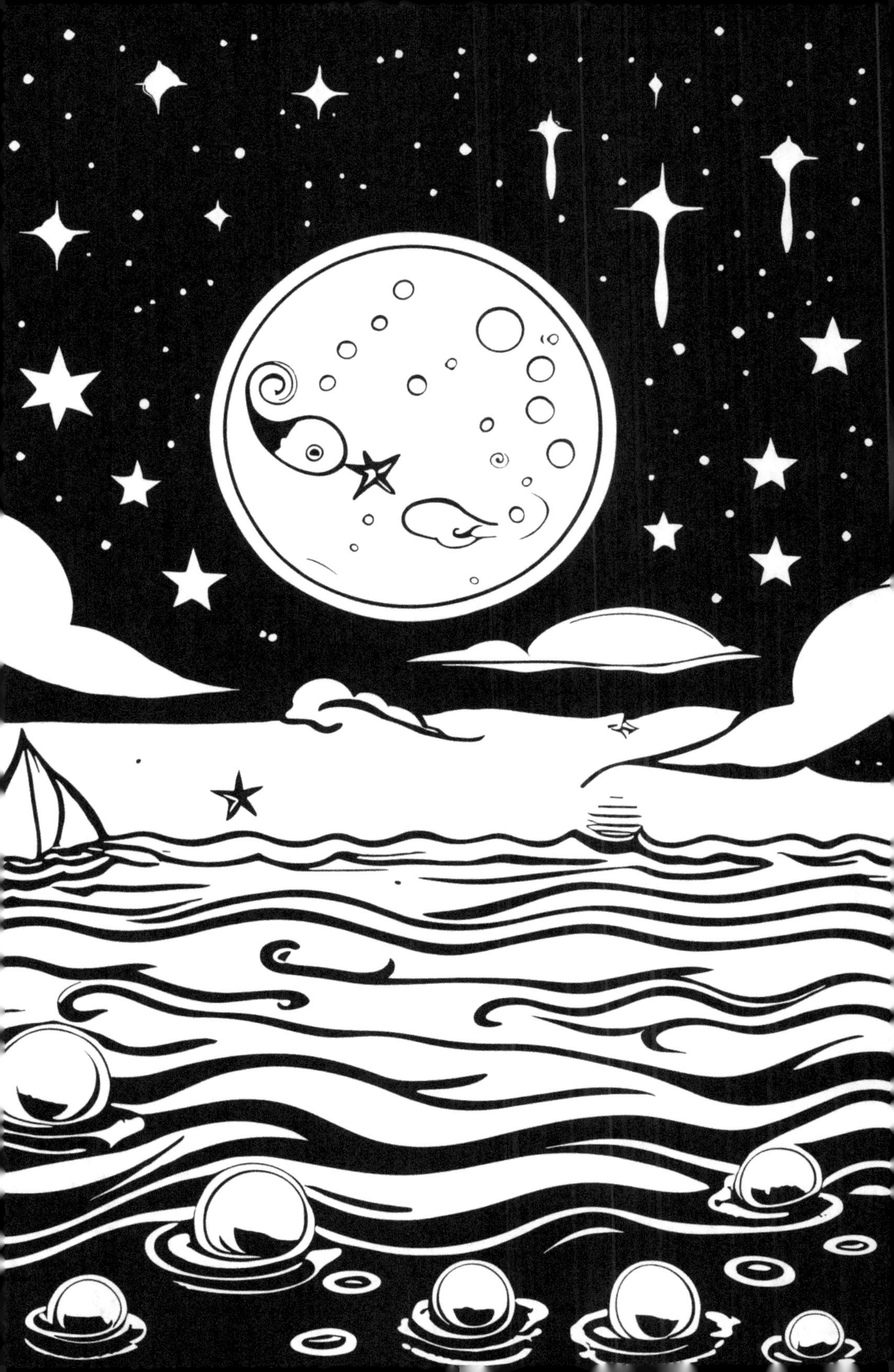

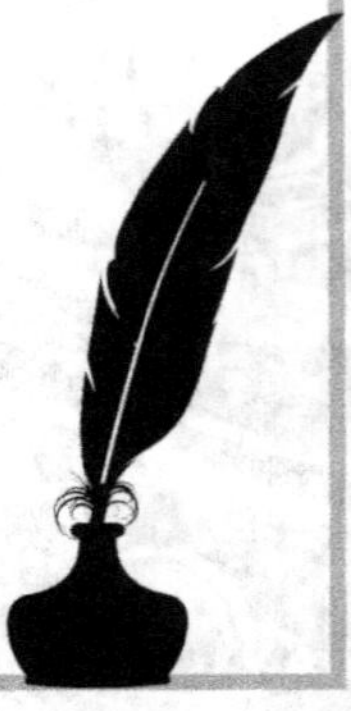

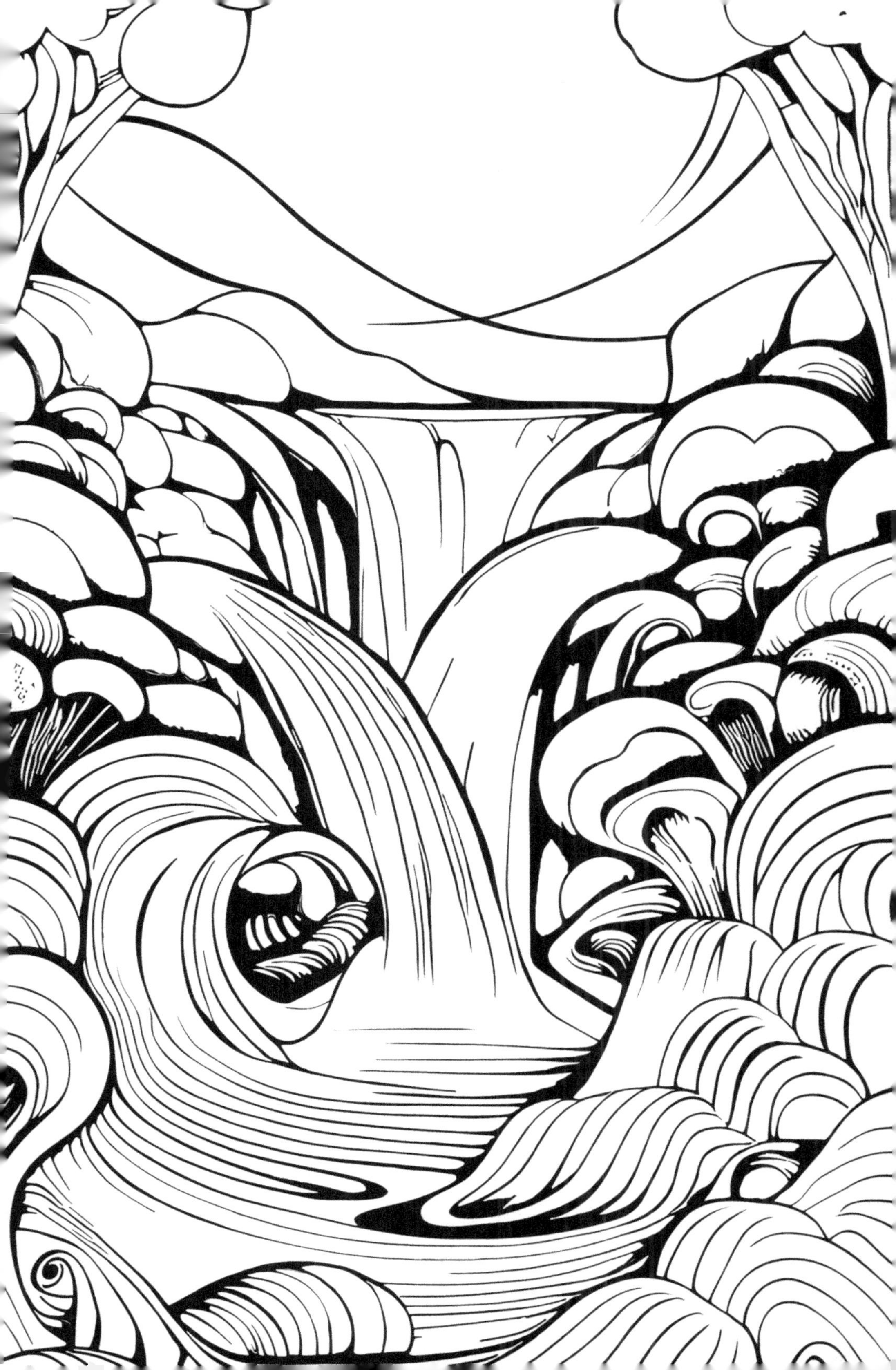

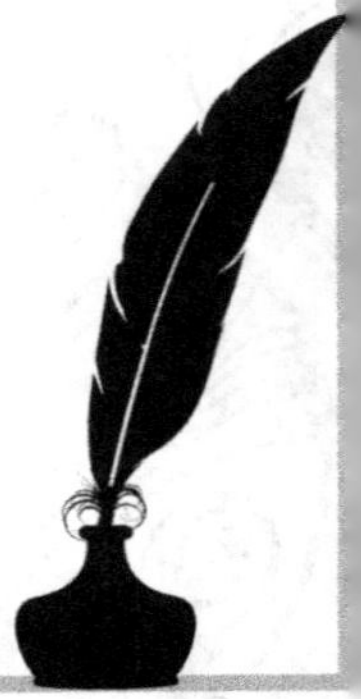

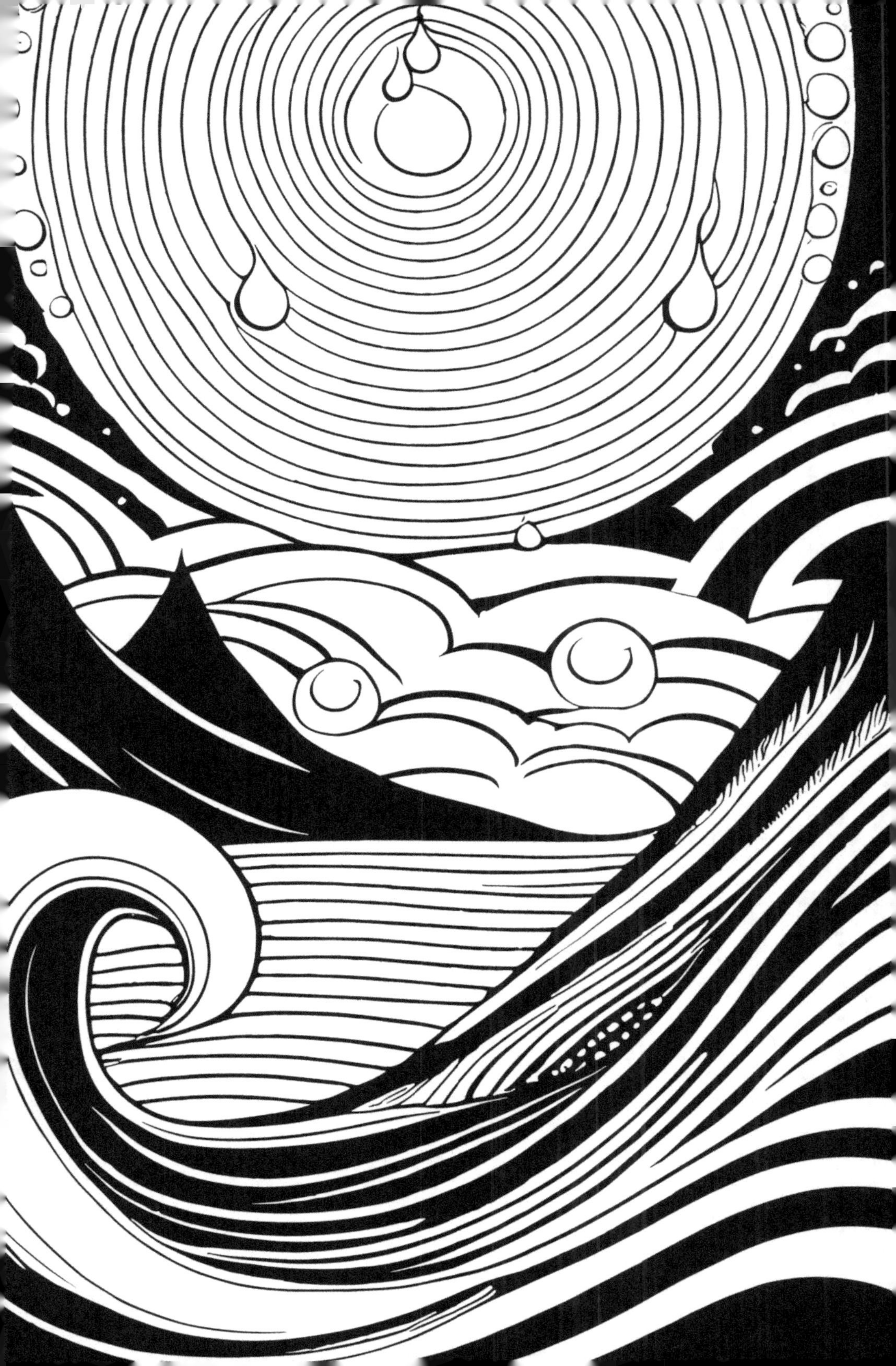

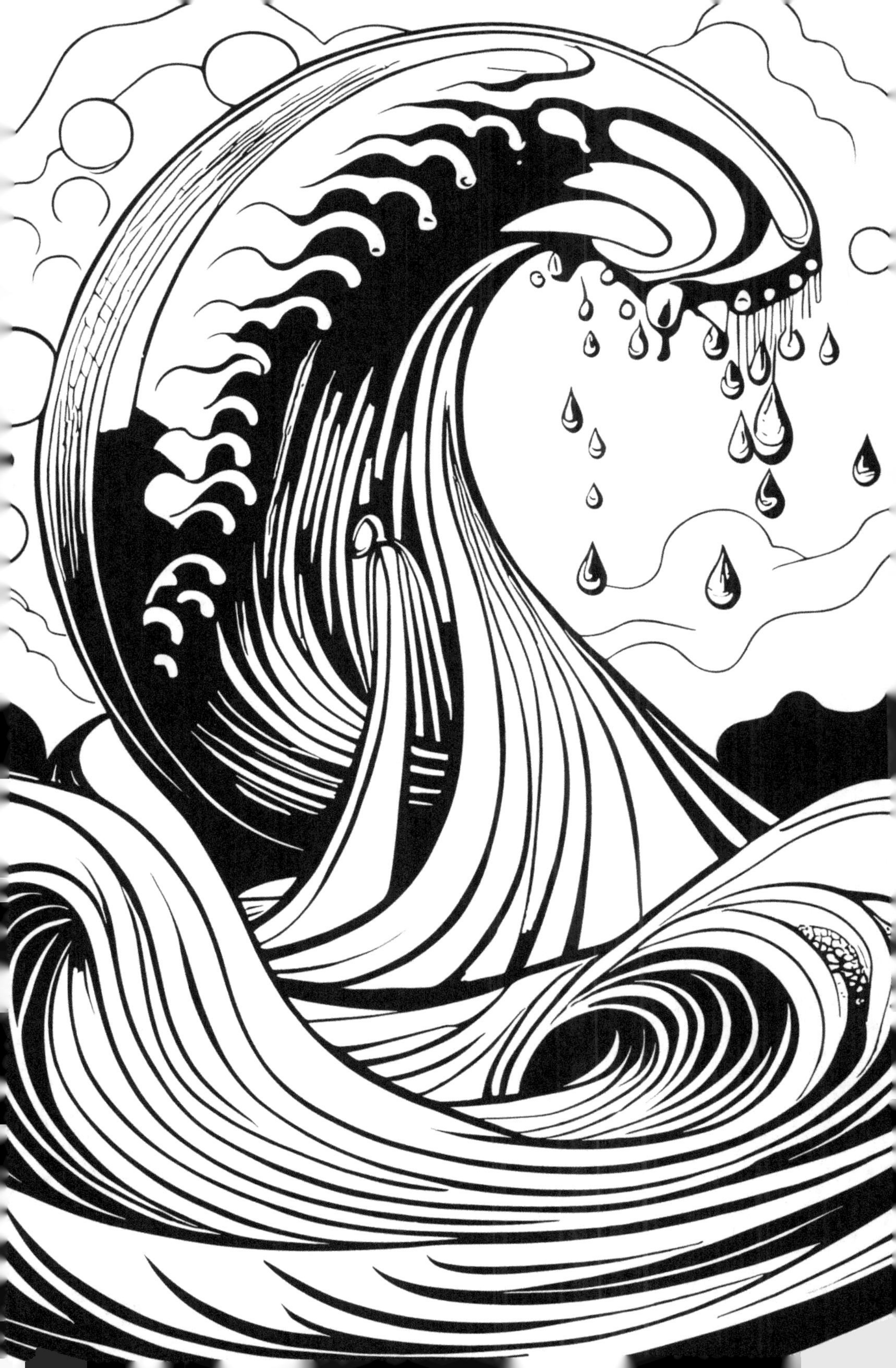

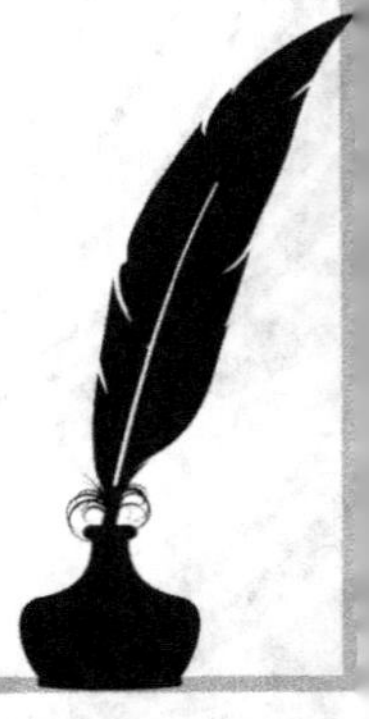

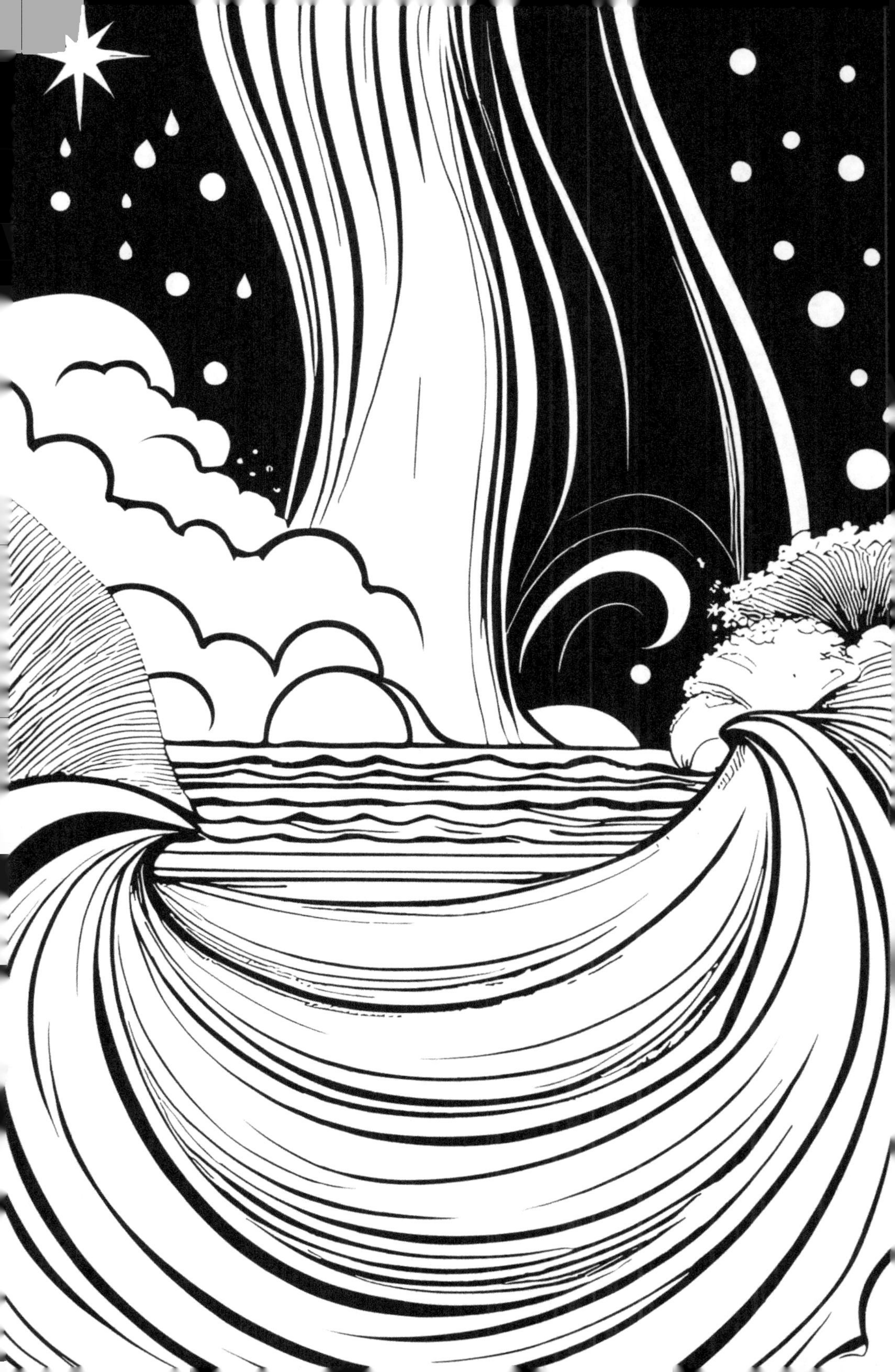

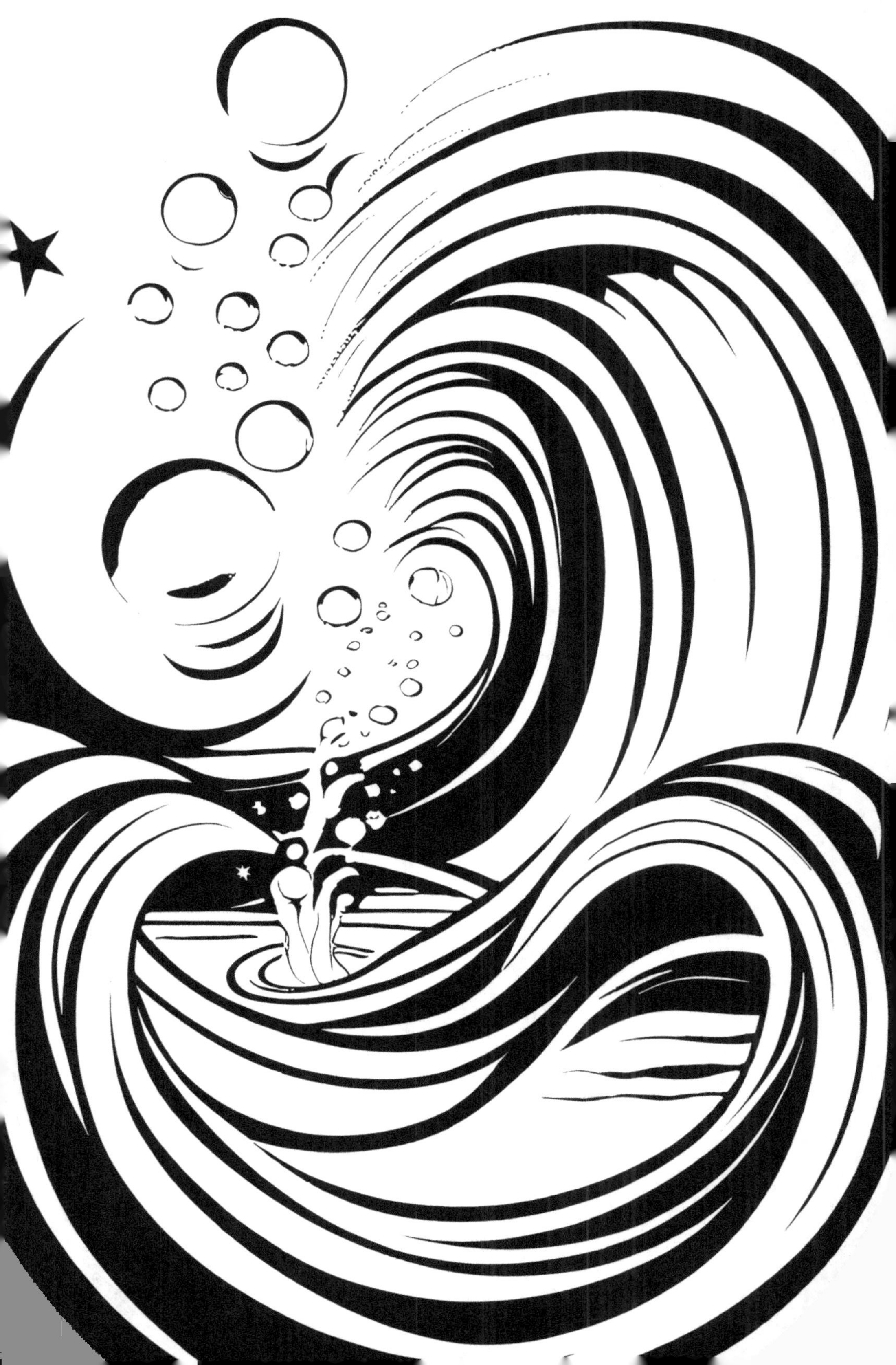

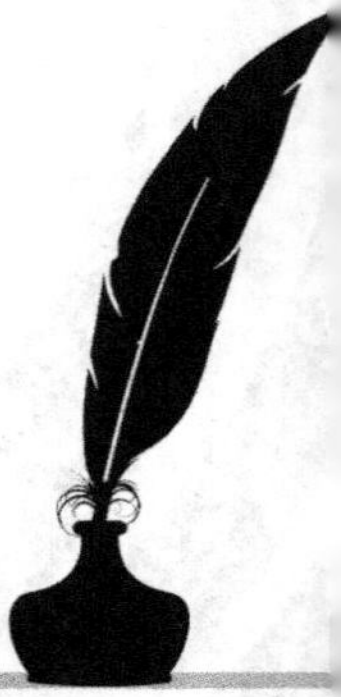

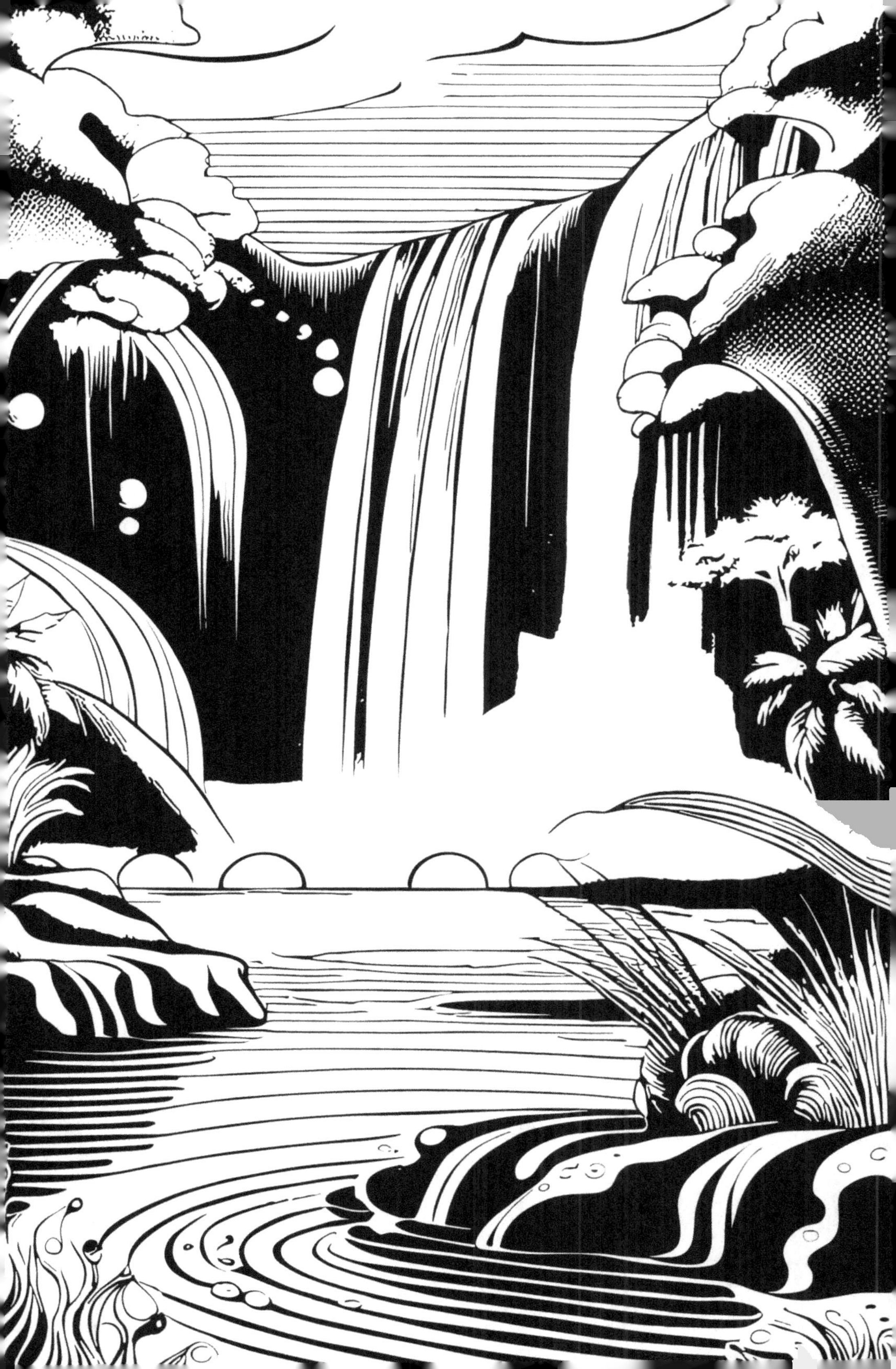

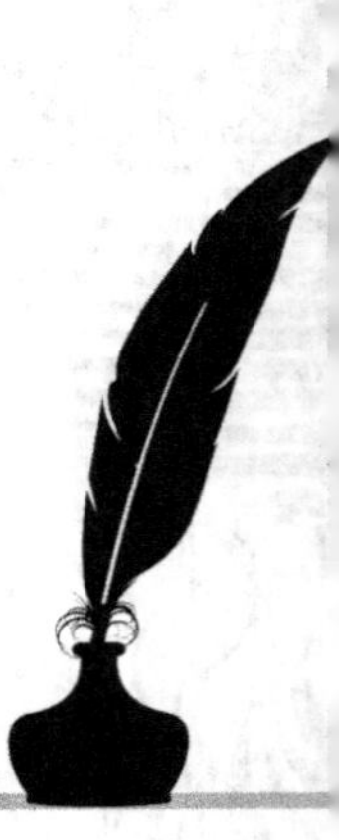

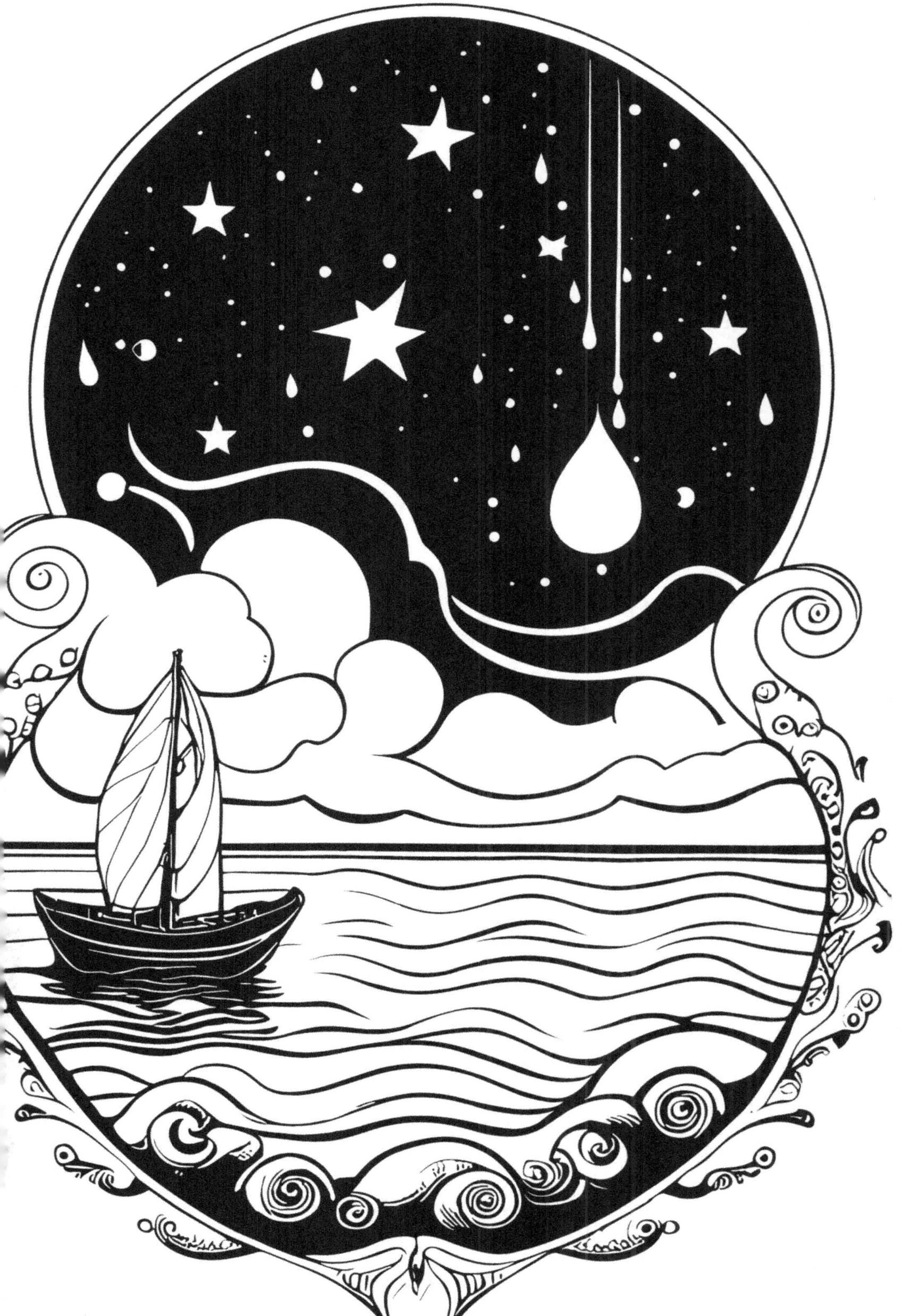

www.ingramcontent.com/pod-product-compliance
Lightning Source LLC
Chambersburg PA
CBHW070116010626
45794CB00013B/2320

* 9 7 9 8 8 6 5 7 2 1 2 0 8 *